HOME RANGE

Writings on Conservation and Restoration

HOME RANGE

Writings on Conservation and Restoration

Kevin Van Tighem

Altitude Publishing

Canadian Rockies / British Columbia / Colorado

Publication Information

Altitude Publishing Canada Ltd.
1500 Railway Avenue, Canmore, Alberta T1W 1P6

Cataloging in Publication Data
Van Tighem, Kevin
Home Range
ISBN 1-55153-912-8
1. Nature conservation. 2. Environmental protection.
3. Conservation of natural resources. 4. Restoration ecology. I. Title.
QH75.V35 2000   333.7'2   C00-911038-0

Printed and bound in Western Canada by Friesens, Altona, Manitoba.

Altitude GreenTree Program

Altitude Publishing will plant twice as many trees as were used in the manufacturing of this product.

We acknowledge the financial support of the Government of Canada through the Book Publishing Industry Development Program (BPIDP) for our publishing activities.

Publisher: Stephen Hutchings
Associate Publisher: Dan Klinglesmith
Design: Stephen Hutchings
Layout: Dan Klinglesmith and Scott Manktelow
Editor: Barbara McCord
Financial Management: Laurie Smith

Contents

Acknowledgements

Making a book takes a lot of work. Time spent writing and assembling it is time not spent doing other things. I am grateful to my family for putting up with the hours I spent typing behind closed doors, and my frequent distractedness when I wasn't writing.

Most people equate writing with authors, but in my experience editors play every bit as important a role. The writer may turn up the occasional gem, but it's the editor who chisels it into a thing of finished worth. It's been my privilege over the years to work with some talented editors who helped me bring earlier versions of the material collected here into print in a number of different publications. I thank, in particular, Margaret Chandler, James Little, John McDermid, Ann Mitchell, David Stalling, Barbara Stevenson and Lynn Zwicky. And, of course, Barbara McCord who edited this book in its entirety.

Dave Petersen: thanks for your sage advice when this book was in its early stages. I took it.

The names of many people appear in the pages that follow. Most, at one time or another, have given generously of their time and knowledge to help me develop these histories and stories. Although too many to list here, I extend my gratitude to all. There could have been no book without you.

Much of this work has appeared in print previously, although each piece has been revised and edited to fit this collection. Thanks to the following periodicals, and their readers, for having given me a voice:

Alberta Fishing Guide: "Yesterday's Fishing Tomorrow," "Tomorrow's Trout," "The Home Stream."

Alberta Outdoorsman: "Licence to Abuse," "Weeds and Wheels," Truly Good People."

Alberta Views: "Troubled Waters."

Bugle: "Real Grizzlies, Real People."

Environment Views: "From Wilds to Weeds," "Fish Without Hooks."

Encompass: "The Grizzly Hunting Placebo."

Outdoor Canada: "The Conservation Century," "Where Wolves Go to Die," "The End of the Hunt?" "Hunting With the Kids," "Man for the Mountains," "The Once and Future Wild."

Outdoor Edge: "Nature Proofing for Allergic Hunters."

Nature Canada: "Toad's Legacy," "Hope on the Range."

Western Sportsman: "Wolves and the Wilds We Hunt."

This book is dedicated, with love and gratitude,
to Gail, Corey, Katie and Brian

Preface

by Bruce Masterman

" *T*hat *land is a community is the basic concept of ecology, but that land is to be loved and respected is an extension of ethics.*"

Aldo Leopold, widely regarded as the father of modern-day scientific wildlife management and ecology, wrote those words in his groundbreaking book A Sand County Almanac on March 4, 1948.

Although more than half a century has passed since then, Leopold's pronouncement holds just as much truth, if not more, now than it did then. The need to love and respect the land, including all living things that call it home, has become recognized as much more than an ethic; in the minds of many people it is a no-brainer, a chance to learn from past mistakes and ensure that the land survives our every attempt to compromise its future.

To many, comprehending the intricate web of life that is nature is a daunting challenge. Some choose to not even try to understand; others, too often those involved in development or resource exploitation, find it easier to deny or fudge the link between habitat and the creatures whose very survival depends on it. Modern media generally don't much help people understand the connections; they are more intent on covering the drama of a brush fire than looking at the bigger picture to reveal that the blaze might actually have been good for the land.

With much of the populace suffering from myopia and/or blurred vision when it comes to conservation matters, it becomes even more critical for those who know how it works to interpret for those who don't. All too often, biologists and land managers are too wrapped up in their battle for bureaucratic survival to take the time to explain to the public the importance of their work in nature's grand scheme. These bureaucrats may be doing great work, but nobody knows about it.

Fortunately, North America has had a rich history of conservation visionaries: people who have made it their mission to explain the intricacies of nature, to help us recognize the links between man and other creatures, to show us that everything we do in our world affects the natural world.

And how we become poorer for every slough drained, forest clearcut and species exterminated.

These visionaries have included the likes of Leopold, Henry David Thoreau, George Bird Grinnell, John Muir and Canada's own Andy Russell and Roderick Haig-Brown.

It's time to add a new name to this austere list: Kevin Van Tighem.

Kevin is a trained biologist. But rather than assume the head-down, introverted stance of many others in his profession, he has chosen to make public education a mission. He does that in speeches, in meeting with people, in his work with Parks Canada and in his passionate writing in books and magazines.

Kevin is a rare breed, one of those lucky souls who has chosen to make his life his livelihood, and vice versa. Fortunately for us, he also is a gifted and passionate writer who can clearly interpret what is going on in the natural world and point out, without sermonizing, how we can minimize our impact on that special world.

In *Home Range*, Kevin details a litany of ecological abuse and mistakes during the first 100 years of settlement in western Canada, including his home province of Alberta. He talks of the ecological perils posed by dams, excessive logging and other resource exploitation, and the reluctance, often driven by fear or myth, to accept other living things such as grizzly bears and wolves. He criticizes engineers who perceive Creation as God's first draft, which can surely be improved on with a little human intervention.

Home Range, however, is not a long-running rant or ecological funeral notice. Quite the contrary; it is a story of hope and optimism. Kevin writes, "Most of us, after all, love this place and mean to stay...And for all the losses ignorance and haste have wrought, much of this land's original living wealth survives. It isn't too late."

For Kevin, hope comes in many forms: recovering populations of bull trout, of ranchers happy to accept grizzlies and wolves as neighbours, of elk once again living along the Milk River in southern Alberta decades after being pushed out, of increasing populations of ducks, bald eagles, peregrine falcons, otters, sandhill cranes and trumpeter swans. He celebrates the victories and the success stories, and laments the losses.

In 1991, I interviewed Kevin after he became president of the Alberta Wilderness Association, a scrappy group not known for being easy on government agencies or politicians whom it perceives as unfriendly toward nature. I asked Kevin how he would balance his role as an employee of Parks Canada with being a vocal advocate for the environment. "I don't see a conflict," he replied. "Both the AWA and Parks Canada are involved in wilderness advocacy." Although his term as president has long finished, Kevin's role as an advocate, both in his official job and in his writing, is stronger than ever.

On a recent September day, I participated in a guided hike that Kevin led along a windswept ridge in Waterton Lakes National Park, where he spent seven years as a conservation biologist before transferring to Jasper National Park. Our band of hikers consisted of writers who specialize in the outdoors. Early in the day, we came upon a bathtub-sized excavation that looked like it had been made by a miniature bulldozer. It was clearly the work of a grizzly bear. Some of us thought the bear had been digging for ground squirrels.

Kevin was quick to unravel the story. The bear, he explained patiently and succinctly, had been doing a little gardening as it fed on sweet vetch, a perennial legume that creates and stores starch in its roots all winter. In late fall and early spring, hungry bears search out sweet vetch for a little carbo-loading. While eating the legumes, the bears at the same time split the remaining roots and cultivate the ground, which stimulates new growth, guaranteeing a future supply.

The hikers looked at each other with mutual amazement. We thought we were a knowledgeable group, but Kevin, without pretence or even a hit of know-it-allness, taught us a lesson we'd never forget.

In Home Range, Kevin delivers many such lessons. He tells us about the special relationship between suckers and harlequin ducks, and how whitewater rafters in Jasper National Park threatened the ducks until Parks Canada restricted rafting. Kevin shows us rivers as living entities. He notes how trout depend on cottonwood trees to deliver leaves to the water, which decompose and provide food for insects, which trout eat.

Van Tighem came by his love for the outdoors early. One of 10 children, he would accompany his father on fishing, hiking, birding and hunting trips throughout southern Alberta. He still fishes and hunts, and credits those activities for giving him special insight into the life requirements of all wild things. While acknowledging that hunters aren't universally popular, Van Tighem makes no apology for being one.

"Almost everything I like about myself goes back, one way or another, to hunting," he writes. "I could never have been so successful a biologist, so passionate an environmentalist or so thoughtful a writer had I never ventured into the wild as a predator."

Just as Aldo Leopold and other great conservationists who hunted were criticized for it, so has Van Tighem. Once, in a speech to a group of naturalists, he spoke of his experiences as a hunter. Afterward, a deeply concerned couple confronted Kevin. They had been Van Tighem fans for years, they said. How, they asked him, could he be such a hypocrite as to profess to care about nature while still being willing to kill animals? The encounter showed Kevin the importance of bridging the intellectual chasm between hunter-naturalists and people who oppose hunting. Both share the same concerns, and for much the same reasons.

In *Home Range*, Van Tighem appeals for mutual acceptance among groups and individuals with diverse opinions—all for the sake of the common ecological good. He encourages people to be better environmental stewards within the larger community of people, while at the same time looking inward at their own relationship with nature to determine where they came from and where they are going.

Kevin calls it coming home. Fairly resonating with grace, passion and eloquence, this book is Van Tighem's personal homecoming.

For those of us to whom the natural world is a life-defining force, not just a casual interest, it couldn't have come at a better time.

Bruce Masterman is a writer who lives in High River, Alberta. He is the author of Heading Out: A Celebration of the Great Outdoors in Calgary and Southern Alberta, *has contributed to three other books and has been published in national and regional magazines and newspapers.*

The Back Trail

From Wilds to Weeds

There were no deer near Strathmore when I was very young. I think I was 12 the first time we saw some—three doe mule deer far out in a field of barley stubble. Dad stopped the car near those exotic creatures so we could watch them in amazement. Dad and Mom grew up in Strathmore, a farming town in southern Alberta. Dad hunted sharp-tailed grouse in the brushy pastures north of town. Mom went fishing with her father on the Bow River near Carseland. It was dry and windy country but even then irrigation was transforming the gently undulating contours of the prairie, as new thickets of cottonwood, willow and saskatoon sprouted where once there had been grassland.

Dad took his children back to the Strathmore area each fall to hunt pheasants on the farms of friends and relatives. Kids have short legs, so the willow and poplar tangles that grew along the edges of the irrigation ditches seemed like jungles to me. It was not until my early teens, however, that those jungles had grown extensive enough for deer to follow the irrigation canals up out of the Bow River valley and make themselves at home on the uplands. By then, poplars that had not yet sprouted when Dad was young were towering veterans, many of them 30 metres tall. One day I pointed out a blue jay to Dad. He was flabbergasted.

Hunting that irrigation country year after year gave me a deep and lasting bond to the land and its wildlife. When the opportunity arose, I studied botany and geography in university.

Listening to Mom and Dad reminisce about the prairies of their youth, I had already begun to realize how much Alberta's prairies had changed in the space of two or three human lifetimes. Even I had seen changes during my few decades: the arrival of deer, then woodpeckers, blue jays, foxes, even the occasional moose. But it was the university library, with its books and journals rich in historical and ecological information, which fully opened my eyes to how much change those familiar everyday fields had known in the past century.

One fall, coming home from another day afield with my now-aging father, we watched stubble burning north of the Trans-Canada Highway. Long lines of flame flickered orange and hungry in the fading evening, scrolling out across the contours of a huge field. I'd been reading about the role that wildfire played in the primeval prairie and suddenly, in the growing darkness when familiar things grow strange, the eyes of my imagination saw past the irrigation country to the wild prairie that had existed here only a few decades earlier.

In my mind's eye I saw an endless, rolling mosaic of needlegrass, blue grama, western wheatgrass and a hundred other species of low-growing grasses, herbs and shrubs stretched out beneath a sky unmarred by jet trails. Great patches of that landscape were blackened where lightning and aboriginal hunters had ignited fires. Tens of thousands of bison peppered the plains, grazing on succulent new grass that had sprouted from earlier burns. The hissing prairie wind was full of their mutter and grumble and the sweet-pungent odour of dung.

In the near distance, a pack of 20 wolves sauntered along the edge of the herd, watching for an opportunity or a sign of weakness. Eagles, ravens and magpies fed on the remains of an old bull nearby. Endless lines of migrating waterfowl-geese, ducks, whooping and sandhill cranes-filled the sky overhead. The prairie echoed with their gabble. Far to the south, a line of gold marked the foliage of cottonwoods along the Bow River where, once in a while, the brilliant green and yellow plumage of Carolina parakeets might even be seen.

The sudden glow of street lamps illuminating a concrete overpass jarred me back to the present; we were arriving home to Calgary, a city that has grown to hold more people than lived in the entire province of Alberta when I was born. I think it was that abrupt return to reality that led me to see, for the first time, the province of my birth as a strange place-where people view landscape change as normal rather than strange and upsetting, where many native plants and animals are endangered while exotics thrive, and whose very landscapes no longer are the product of place but of artifice.

What has happened to the west? Where is home?

Two centuries ago, few of the people who lived here minded when rivers flooded in the spring. They simply got out of the way and waited for the flow to ebb. Meltwaters filled each hollow and gully with wetlands—big wetlands in wet years and smaller ones in dry years. During the dry summer and fall months when fires swept the landscape, people and wildlife simply moved aside and waited for them to pass. The landscape contained no straight lines, only curving ones. Wildlife abounded.

Alberta's ecosystems depended on natural cycles and periodic disturbances to keep them vital. Floods fertilized and watered riparian (river-bottom) areas, regularly renewing lush tangles of cottonwood and sandbar willow. Wet cycles refilled potholes and wetlands, while dry spells expanded shorelines. Waterfowl benefited from the wet, while piping plovers and other shorebirds often benefited from the dry. Fires created new forage for grazing animals and, in wooded areas, maintained a constantly shifting mosaic of vegetation from old forests through to shrubby, open burns.

Aboriginal people understood those natural forces; that was simply how their world was. They knew that many bison would drown each spring in the swollen floodwaters of prairie rivers and that there would be good hunting in the aftermath of forest and prairie fires as new greenery sprouted out of blackened landscapes. Wolves and ravens were their companions in the hunt. When the berries ripened in the coulees they shared them, warily, with silver-tipped bears.

Those natural processes had free play on the sprawling young landscapes that emerged from beneath glacier ice 12,000 years or so ago. As plants and animals from more distant parts of the continent gradually colonized the western plains, foothills and mountains, fire, flood, drought and weather moulded them into a new ecological mosaic. Humans and animals alike co-evolved with the western landscape. By the 18th century, the ecological diversity of Alberta's grasslands, wetlands, forests and mountain landscapes supported unimaginable numbers of animals, each with its own habitats and its own ways of making a living.

In 1754 change arrived. It wore a white face, side whiskers and, no doubt, a bemused expression. That year Anthony Henday, the first European to describe what would someday become Alberta, looked west from somewhere near modern-day Carstairs and saw what he described as the Shining Mountains. Then he turned back east to report to his fur trade superiors, setting in motion forces that would rearrange the face of that landscape at a pace and on a scale greater than anything that had ever come before.

Soon after, the Hudson's Bay Company and Northwest Company established fur trading outposts along the Athabasca and North Saskatchewan rivers. By the time ranchers began to speculate on Alberta grass in the late 1800s, the west had already become a place of plunder and slaughter. Beavers were the first resource to attract the get-rich-quick enthusiasm of European capitalists. Many populations of beavers and other furbearers were extirpated by the late 1800s. As beaver populations crashed, their dams washed out and wetland areas shrank all across the north and through the foothills.

The growing numbers of fur traders, prospectors, missionaries and other European frontiersmen relied on aboriginal people to supply them with big game, ducks, geese, grouse and other game. First Nations hunters, already exceptionally skilled, became deadly once equipped with modern firearms. By the beginning of the 20th century uncontrolled slaughter by European and aboriginal hunters had virtually wiped out most accessible game populations to feed growing towns, mining camps, logging camps and other outposts. Elk survived only in a few small herds that ranged the upper Brazeau and Kananaskis valleys. Accessible streams were depleted of their original abundance of bull and cutthroat trout. Whooping cranes and trumpeter swans no longer nested in the aspen parkland. Bison were only memories.

Wildlife populations were so low that Canada's Minister of the Interior, worried that tourists to the nation's new park at Banff might be disappointed, commissioned a study by Mr. W.F. Whitcher. Whitcher concluded that market hunting had nearly wiped out game. He recommended the government kill off predators to save the survivors. In reality, however, predator populations had already been decimated by strychnine, traps and unregulated hunting.

By 1900, then, Alberta's wildlife wealth had been devastated. A growing flood of aggressive colonists was spilling across the land. Few, if any, of those newcomers had any experience that would help them begin to understand the ecosystems they appropriated for their own use. They extirpated bison, vultures and plains grizzlies, nearly eradicated elk and beavers, and hunted waterfowl year-round. Even scavengers felt their impact. The black-billed magpie was among many species unable to resist feeding at poisoned wolf and coyote baits; accounts describe magpies as rare, and ravens unheard of.

An awful silence settled across a land that, only a few decades earlier, had teemed with life.

Even as government began to waken to the need to conserve wildlife populations by bringing in closed seasons and controls on hunting, the tide of settlement began a far more long-lasting set of changes to Alberta's ecosystems and wildlife—habitat loss.

It was the Canadian Pacific Railway that kicked off the first great wave of change to wash across Alberta since the Ice Age. Upon its arrival in Alberta in 1883, the big steel rail suddenly made it easy for hopeful settlers to travel west, lay claim to a homestead and build new lives as farmers and ranchers. Wheels shrink distance, so the prairies overnight ceased to be the barrier they had been previously.

Those hopeful farmers had a problem, however. The same natural forces that give life to Alberta's natural ecosystems work against efforts to settle and crop the land. Fires burn fields, fences and homes. Droughts breed grasshoppers and dry out crops. Wet cycles make it impossible to work the land with machinery. Floods kill livestock, damage buildings and wreak havoc on towns and cities.

The 20th century, consequently, saw a progression of government and community initiatives to eliminate those natural processes. Fire control, dams, wetland drainage and irrigation were among the chief methods.

By the 1930s, thanks to cultivated fields and a spreading gridwork of roads, big prairie fires had become pretty much a thing of the past. Forest fire control only became effective in the 1950s with the growing use of aircraft to water-bomb remote blazes.

As fires became less frequent, aspen forests spread south and east into areas that had formerly been grassland. Stettler-area naturalist Lloyd Lohr describes the landscape around his Stettler farm at the time his grandfather first homesteaded the area in 1900: "There were groves of trees, but there was a lot of grass and a lot of sloughs. There'd be a slough and then a circle of willows and then maybe some bigger poplars around it...but prairie fires came through every spring and sometimes in the fall...They would burn up to these bushes, burn the grass and then they would kill the sapling trees around the ring. And the bigger trees in the middle, they'd stay. So it kept it under control that way."

Today, dense aspen forests surround Lloyd's farm. White-tailed deer, non-existent when his grandfather arrived, are everywhere. The aspen forests provide them with safe cover, no wolves or cougars survive to eat them, and fields of alfalfa and grain provide a rich food supply. Native birds like upland sandpipers, Sprague's pipits and sharp-tailed grouse, part of the fabric of Lloyd's boyhood, are rare. Starlings, savannah sparrows, ruffed grouse and Hungarian partridges—species better suited for life in the new landscape-have replaced them.

Settlers welcomed floods no more than fires, especially since many Alberta towns and cities originated where trails crossed creeks and rivers. Calgary, Rockyford, Okotoks, High River, Red Deer and Lethbridge all had to deal with spring floodwaters that washed away buildings, livestock and the occasional hapless human.

Spring floods too often gave way to summer droughts. Farmers who had watched vast quantities of water pouring off the landscape in May and June had to contend with hot sun, cloudless skies and moisture-sucking winds during July and August when their growing crops most needed water.

Alistair Crerar, executive director of the now-defunct Environment Council of Alberta, once wrote: "Water in a dry land has a mythic emotive power that moves civil engineers to visions and irrigation farmers to poetry. The absence or shortage of water is so searing, so terrifying, that anything that promises to prevent or avoid it is accepted without question."

As towns grew and farms proliferated, demand for control of Alberta's undisciplined streams and rivers increased. From 1950 on, governments built a series of huge dams to tame Alberta rivers for irrigation water supply, power and flood control. In the late 1960s the immense WAC Bennett Dam in British Columbia tamed even the mighty Peace River.

Big dams produced big reservoirs, which, while popular with migrating waterfowl seeking to avoid hunters' guns, produce little in the way of fish or wildlife habitats. Most reservoirs, unlike natural lakes, fill during fall, winter and spring, and drain during summer. Few plants or animals can adapt to such a backward ecosystem, so our big reservoirs support only bottom-feeding or deepwater fish and, along their shorelines, exotic weeds.

Big dams release water that is several degrees above freezing point, so river reaches downstream from the dams remain ice-free all winter long. Geese, ducks and other birds that once had no choice but to migrate south now winter in Alberta by the thousands, resting on the open waters of dammed rivers, and feeding with cattle in feedlots or scavenging the remains of grain crops in stubble fields. Bald eagles, peregrine falcons and other predators that once followed the flocks south sometimes winter here now too. Although the increase in wintering waterfowl might be seen as an enrichment of Alberta's living environment, dams have created an ongoing legacy of loss too. By disrupting spring floods and cutting off supplies of silt and gravel from upstream, big dams have contributed to gradual reductions in the numbers of cottonwood trees and other plants that need spring flooding to create their preferred habitats. Many hundreds of kilometres of wildlife habitat downstream from Alberta's dams have been degraded or lost.

Running parallel with the control of fire and water in Alberta was an expansion of cultivated farmland. Land that wasn't growing crops was considered "unimproved"; most of Alberta's former grasslands have now been "improved" for agriculture. By the 1970s it was already difficult to find native grassland in the most fertile parts of the province—the aspen parkland region that extends from Lloydminster to Edmonton and south to Drumheller and High River. Today, ecologists who have studied aerial photography and satellite images of Alberta estimate that less than one percent of the original fescue grassland survives in central Alberta. Not even one-fifth of the drier grassland types have escaped the plough.

To bring more land into production for grains and other crops, governments provided programs and subsidies to drain wetlands. The result was a steady, irreversible loss of the most productive habitat for waterfowl, amphibians and other wildlife, and further changes to the movement of water across the prairie and parkland landscapes. Gradually the rich mosaic of low-lying sedge marshes, sprawling wetlands, shortgrass ridge tops and mixed-grass uplands that once typified prairie Alberta has given way to a checkerboard of monocultures that feed no bison, shelter no pipits and provide habitat for only a few common wildlife species.

By the 1970s irrigation farming had spread across most of the region between Calgary, Medicine Hat and the Milk River Ridge. Today, more than two-thirds of all the irrigated farmland in Canada is in Alberta. Rivers like the lower Bow and Oldman run so nearly dry in summer that fish sometimes die, but the once-dry uplands are lush and green with exotic crops watered by an intricate network of canals and pipelines.

The irrigation projects and farms of the early part of this century produced windbreaks, shrub tangles and woodlands across the land where the bison once roamed. Blackbirds, orioles, pheasants, deer and other animals that could adapt to these patchwork habitats thrived in the new irrigation farming landscapes. The rest—animals like wolves, elk, burrowing owls and upland sandpiper that depend on fires, floods, native vegetation or isolation-vanished or became rare.

In the 1980s, the Alberta government began to pour hundreds of millions of oil royalty dollars into projects to make irrigation canals more efficient. This meant, among other things, killing off the poplar forests and brush tangles that lined the leaky old canals. As farms grew larger and farmers moved to town, many of the old farmsteads with their windbreaks and shelterbelts vanished too. Few parts of Alberta have seen as much ecological change as irrigation country. The loss of natural diversity continues today. Offsetting the losses, to some degree, is the increased number of artificial wetlands created by some of Alberta's more enlightened irrigation districts. Some birds like glossy ibis and black-crowned night heron-once unknown in Alberta-have spread north from the U.S. to take up residence in these productive wetlands. Northern birds like white pelicans, double-crested cormorants and terns now nest on islands in large irrigation reservoirs like McGregor Lake. For the most part, however, southern Alberta's prairies are biological disaster areas; depleted ghosts of the once-vital ecosystems they were only a century ago.

In the 1980s the control of nature and remaking of landscapes spread north into the northern forests, in response to government subsidies to the pulp and paper industry. Already sliced by hundreds of thousands of kilometres of oil industry exploration cutlines, northern forests, muskegs, wetlands and river meadows are now rapidly giving way to a network of roads connecting clearcut expanses of scarified (ploughed) soil planted to commercial tree species. Logging, unlike fire, does not enrich the landscape with phosphorus-rich ash, deadfall, standing snags, and an abundance of down and standing deadwood later to be colonized by ants, beetles and other animals. As a result, the industrialization of northern Alberta has already begun to eliminate sensitive species like caribou, marten and boreal wood warblers, while creating the patchwork, disturbed landscapes favoured by weedy species like white-tailed deer, coyote, cowbird and starling.

The 20th century was barely half over before many people in North America awakened to the realization that wilderness, many native wildlife species, and the clean water and air that we had previously taken for granted were disappearing. Even oil-rich, optimistic Albertans began to see their province as a place of endangered species and vanishing natural ecosystems. Organizations like the Alberta Wilderness Association and Federation of Alberta Naturalists became active in promoting the need for nature conservation.

By the 1980s support for conservation was widespread in Alberta, even if government action was reluctant at best. Battles over the Oldman River Dam, northern pulp mills and industrial tourism development in Banff National Park awakened more and more Albertans to the fact that their province's natural wealth could no longer be taken for granted.

Reluctantly, in the 1990s, Alberta's anti-environment government gave in to widespread public demand to protect what little remained of Alberta's original wild beauty. The few small patches of landscape that finally gained recognition through the province's notorious "Special Places" program remained open to many of the industrial uses that most parks and protected areas elsewhere prohibit. Even if they had been properly protected, however, the question of restoring their ecological vitality would have been perplexing. After a century of constant change, expanding settlement and control of nature, few Albertans can begin to imagine what our ecosystems should look like under natural conditions, or how to restore the natural processes needed to restore some of our province's native diversity. At the end of the day, if we fail to restore natural fire and flood regimes, bring back wild predators and change livestock grazing patterns to more closely reflect what the native vegetation is adapted to, even the best-protected areas will continue changing away from their natural condition.

Animals whose ecology was ideally suited for the conditions that prevailed in pristine Alberta but not for eluding human predators were the first to decline as human numbers increased through the late 1800s and early 1900s. With better wildlife regulations and more public concern for conservation of game animals, some of those animal species have recovered. Deer, for example, once virtually eradicated south of the Bow River, are now widespread and abundant. Trumpeter swans, bull trout and even whooping cranes are more numerous than they used to be.

However, even as Alberta began to conserve and restore animals once threatened by uncontrolled hunting, we continued to change their habitat directly—through agricultural expansion, the growth of cities and the expansion of industries like forestry, and indirectly—by putting out fire, controlling the flows of rivers and streams, and draining wetlands.

Today, the amount of green hasn't changed much, but fewer kinds of plants contribute to it. The total number of animals remains high, but most are domestic or weedy species. Ecologically, Alberta has become a poor facsimile of itself.

Native wildlife that thrive in Alberta's man-made habitats are those like deer, horned larks, kestrels, willows and others that can find food and shelter in a man-made ecological mosaic and that are tolerated by, or able to hide from, humans. Those that have declined—like piping plovers, burrowing owls, curlews and grizzly bears—depend on habitats sustained by natural processes we've altered, need habitats we've destroyed or fragmented, or are those we simply refuse to tolerate or protect.

Looking for hope and inspiration in the post-frontier west is a daunting challenge. Humans are more numerous than ever before; our mark is everywhere. Compounding our sheer numbers is our collective determination to enjoy a high material standard of living, and our general scarcity of ecological literacy and direct contact with wild nature.

Even so, there may yet be more cause for hope than despair that we will find ways to restore what is most real, and best, about this unique place on Earth. Most of us, after all, love this place and mean to stay. Science has given us deeper insights into the workings of nature than ever before in human history. History has taught us practical lessons about what doesn't work, and what might. And for all the losses ignorance and haste have wrought, much of this land's original living wealth survives. It isn't too late.

Since Anthony Henday, generations of outsiders have flowed into Alberta, leaving home behind and imposing foreign ambitions on a landscape they did not know or recognize. This was not their home range—but it has come to be ours. That is why we owe it to ourselves to better understand the nature of this wounded place we call home, and to put that understanding to work in restoring as much of its health and diversity as possible. It's time to find our way home.

Troubled Waters

Soon after his 1876 arrival at the confluence of the Bow and Elbow rivers, Northwest Mounted Police Commissioner Irvine proposed that the new fort be called Calgary "...which I believe is 'Scotch' for 'Clear Running Water,' a very appropriate name I think." The Bow River I grew up beside a century later differed from the wild stream that greeted those first NWMP officers. Spring ice jams and floods threatened their fort among the Bow's cottonwood groves. By my time, however, downtown Calgary confidently occupied the river's floodplain, protected from floods by upstream dams. Irvine's river ran faintly blue with glacial silt in midsummer, shrinking and clearing as fall drew near. My river flowed more evenly through the seasons; its flow regulated by dams whose reservoirs also trapped glacial silt, making the river clearer than in Irvine's day. NWMP Corporal Denny, whose letters home provide a fine record of frontier Calgary life, fished for fat cutthroat and bull trout in the river's eddies and beneath its many log jams. I fished beneath the Crowchild Bridge for exotic rainbow and brown trout, the natives long ago having been fished out. Logjams and young cottonwoods were rare.

It was still the Bow River—but a different river altogether.

We Albertans tend to take our rivers for granted. They flow through our lives virtually unnoticed. We have little sense of how they have changed in response to the ambitions and choices of those who built our province—and perhaps too little concern about how our own choices might affect those rivers and the people who will live beside them tomorrow.

Our complacency belies the fact that we are, far more than many realize, a river people. Our earliest settlements grew up beside rivers. Some, like Edmonton, Rocky Mountain House and Athabasca, were at strategic stopping places for boat parties. Others, like High River, Calgary, Red Deer and Rockyford, rose where overland trails converged on shallow fords or safe crossings. Today's urban parks line city riverfronts. Anglers flock to the famous lower Bow, Crowsnest, North Raven and Ram rivers. Kayakers play in eddies on the Oldman, Kananaskis and Brazeau. Freighting boats still ply the Peace, Athabasca and Slave. Kids skip rocks or dream as they watch the passing water. Ranch buildings and campgrounds shelter beneath riverside spruce and cottonwoods.

A decade ago, Albertans were more river-conscious than today. Public concern about Alberta rivers peaked in the late 1980s after the provincial government began to authorize increased industrial development. The first sign of serious problems down by the waterside was in 1986, when fish began dying in the Highwood and Elbow rivers. Then, in 1987, in the face of widespread and vocal opposition, the Alberta government began construction of a dam on the Oldman River near Pincher Creek. Controversy over river conservation remained focused in the south until 1988 when the government announced eight major pulp mill projects in northern Alberta. Suddenly northerners faced the prospect of tonnes of organic waste, laced with cancer-causing dioxins, furans and other organochlorines, pouring into the Athabasca, Wapiti and Peace rivers. The resulting wave of public outrage caught provincial politicians off-guard. In the 1989 provincial election, that outrage showed up at the polls; although voters returned the ruling Tories to power, both Environment Minister Ian Reid and Premier Don Getty went down to defeat partly because of their record on environmental issues. Getty turned to Stettler-area voters—far from both the Oldman and the northern pulp mills—to elect him in a subsequent by-election.

Pulp mills and dams were supposed to be good news stories. The angry public reaction sent a forceful message not only to politicians but also to Alberta Environment's powerful water bureaucracy: Albertans wanted our rivers treated as something better than plumbing systems.

In 1989 the University of Calgary hosted a conference, Flowing to the Future, that brought together environmental advocates, government resource planners, special-interest groups and others concerned about the future of Alberta's rivers. The conference, and a follow-up conference two years later at the University of Alberta, generated recommendations to protect rivers. But by 1991 the Oldman Dam was finished and filled, the pulp mills were up and running and the province's economy had gone sour. Public concern about environmental issues gave way to financial worries.

The rivers still flowed to the future, but people no longer noticed.

Alberta rivers are ill-disciplined things. Spring rains swell their flow until they are brown and heavy, hissing sullenly among the trees and shrubs of their floodplains. Ten to 20 times more water flows downstream during spring floods than in midwinter when headwater valleys lie frozen beneath the snow. Rivers in the South Saskatchewan drainage—most of southern Alberta, in other words—pass up to 60 percent of their flow in May and June.

Spring floods can be formidable. Early explorers described bison dying by the hundreds while crossing flood-swollen prairie rivers. A 1995 flood caused millions of dollars of property damage in the Oldman River basin. Such abundance of water, however, is long gone by July and August when farmers' fields bake beneath the midsummer sun. In prairie Alberta, where crops often wither for lack of water, thirsty summer memories of wasted spring runoff have inspired a century's worth of dam projects.

Northern Alberta rivers inspire local boosters to lobby for taxpayer-funded dams too, but for different reasons. The most common complaint in the north is not too little water in summer, but too much in spring. Communities beside northern rivers face frequent flooding.

Such seasonal extremes, however, are what run a river's ecosystem. Trout rely on heavy spring flows to stimulate their upstream migrations to headwater spawning beds. Cottonwood trees and sandbar willows release seeds in June, just in time for those seeds to sprout on newly deposited sandbars where receding floodwaters irrigate their fast-growing seedling roots. The slackened flows of autumn capture billions of fresh-fallen leaves and carry them lazily into quiet eddies. Those decomposing leaves feed battalions of caddisfly, mayfly and midge larvae through the winter when other food is scarce. They, in turn, feed fish, frogs and mink. The entire river ecosystem is adapted to, and needs, the seasonal cycle of violent flood and sleepy near-drought that so frustrates our human desire for a stable environment.

Conversely, of course, the dams we build to smooth out those seasonal flows throw the natural world into confusion. Fish can no longer migrate. Cottonwood seeds lodge on dry sand and die. Tamed rivers can no longer rearrange their channels and revitalize their floodplains. Instead, they become entrenched—especially when further confined by flood-control dikes and armoured with riprapped banks.

Because a river's plants and animals live in intimate contact with the water, whatever is in the water soon works its way into the ecosystem. The convenient thing about flowing water, from a human standpoint, is that it's always going elsewhere. That makes it easy to dispose of unwanted wastes: simply pour them in the river. Alberta's oil industry was once a major polluter of rivers like the Bow and North Saskatchewan. Although the petroleum industry has cleaned up its act to a remarkable degree, cities and pulp mills continue to contaminate Alberta's rivers.

At the Flowing to the Future conferences, ecologists talked with Cree hunters, environmentalists argued with industry scientists and Alberta Environment's well-paid and powerful water engineers debated with everyone. For a while it seemed like a new, more enlightened vision of river conservation might emerge from the unprecedented sharing of knowledge and perspective. But then the conferences ended.

As the 20th century gives way to the 21st, the uproar over Alberta's rivers seems to have abated. Our demands on them, however, have not. Despite some progress, few involved in river conservation issues express much confidence in the future.

Kerry Brewin is senior fisheries biologist for Trout Unlimited Canada, a conservation group consisting mostly of anglers who work to protect cold-water ecosystems. Mr. Brewin notes that after the river conferences the province of Alberta finally replaced its long-outdated Water Resources Act with a new Water Act that includes potentially useful new tools for protecting rivers. The old legislation, modelled on the century-old Northwest Irrigation Act, was designed only to promote water development, not protect rivers. It allocated water for "beneficial uses"—all of them outside the riverbed.

Alberta's 1999 Water Act reflects the public environmental concern that emerged in response to the older law's destructive legacy. The Act allows government to reserve water for rivers and mandates development of a strategy to "protect the aquatic environment." It promotes watershed management by linking land use planning with water planning, and guarantees public involvement in major river decisions. The Act prohibits major diversions of water from one river basin into another-a radical shift in policy from two decades ago when water engineers were building the Dickson Dam on the Red Deer and the Three Rivers Dam on the Oldman in places where they could be used for future north-to-south water transfers.

Still, says TU's Brewin, the new Water Act's conservation provisions are vague and, too often, discretionary. For example, the Minister "may" develop water management plans, which "may" be done consultatively and in a way that integrates land use considerations. On the other hand, of course, the Minister may choose not do any of those and be fully compliant with the Act. The language is permissive rather than mandatory.

Rivers need guaranteed instream flows, for example, to ensure that fish can swim and breath, streamside vegetation will have wet roots, and productive riparian ecosystems will remain lush, especially during the critical midsummer season. Where human users have licensed rights to most of a river's natural flow, government-reserved water for the river itself is critically important. The new Water Act makes this possible, at last. However, Mr. Brewin says, "There are no timelines for any of this stuff. If things like instream flows are ever implemented, good things could happen."

For some rivers it may already be too late. According to University of Lethbridge ecologist Stewart Rood, so much of the St. Mary River's flow is already devoted to irrigation use that water planners could only bring themselves to increase its minimum flow from the paltry 0.93 cubic metres per second that it got in the 1980s to 2.75 cubic metres per second today. Pointing out that most of the St. Mary's cottonwood trees are already dead, Dr. Rood describes the river's ecosystem as "collapsed."

"With the St. Mary we have to talk about restoration, not protection," he says. "Without more water, the prognosis for the St. Mary is bad."

In spite of this, Rood is optimistic about prospects for river conservation. His studies on floodplain cottonwood forests led Alberta Environment to adopt a "flow ramping" strategy for the Oldman Dam, an approach since adopted for the St. Mary and other dams. Flow ramping allows a dam to capture spring runoff and store it for summer use in downstream irrigation farms, but tries to mimic the natural river flow pattern by releasing a moderate spring flood and then gradually reducing the flow into early summer. Dr. Rood believes that floodplain vegetation suffers more from sudden changes in water availability than from the reduced intensity of spring floods. Besides, he points out, until the Oldman's modified flow is totally used up by irrigators (which could happen within a decade) the downstream ecosystem will enjoy more water than before the dam, when the river's natural summer flow was sucked nearly dry.

"I've seen the Oldman down to one cubic metre per second at Fort Macleod and five at Lethbridge," he says. "The minimum flow now is 20 cubic metres per second at Lethbridge."

Dr. Rood was a member of a multi-stakeholder committee that the Alberta government established to advise on how to operate the Oldman Dam. Although dominated by irrigation lobbyists, the Oldman River Dam Environmental Advisory Committee quickly agreed that the river's health could no longer be compromised. The committee reviewed Alberta water law and discovered that the dam, ironically, may provide a legal angle for protecting river flows. Before the dam, the Oldman's natural flow was governed by a traditional "first-in-time, first-in-right" doctrine that gave precedence to the oldest water licences. Now, however, downstream from the dam, the Oldman has more than just its natural flow in summer. Water released from its reservoir is stored, not natural, water. This means that any summer flows above what would naturally exist need not go to senior water licensees like the large St. Mary, Taber and Lethbridge Northern Irrigation Districts who are entitled only to "natural" water. Some of the stored water can be reserved for urban water needs and protecting river ecosystems.

Sharing water shortages fairly, rather than giving the oldest water licences all the water they want while leaving junior licensees—and the river—to do without, is a fair and rational approach. It's also a radical departure from traditional practice, and threatens the once-firm grip on water and economic power the region's politically dominant irrigation compact has enjoyed. That may be why the committee's recommendation remains stalled in Edmonton. Without significant public pressure, and in the face of powerful special interests, the government has dragged its feet rather than risk doing the right thing.

As evidence that government water managers are better at making promises than delivering results, Kerry Brewin points to official foot-dragging on even so simple a matter as screening the mouths of irrigation canals. Farm irrigation districts divert well more than 2.6 million cubic decametres of water each year out of rivers in the South Saskatchewan watershed. Countless fish get drawn out of rivers into the irrigation canals each summer. In the fall, when irrigation engineers turn off the flow, those fish are trapped and die. Brewin and other TU volunteers rescued almost 70,000 fish from irrigation canals downstream from Calgary in 1999. Despite well-orchestrated media coverage and lobbying, the government has yet to screen the diversion canals.

"I found reports dating back to 1911 and 1912 saying that fish losses were a problem due to lack of fish screens," Brewin says. "We called for a provincial task force to solve the problem of fish losses in irrigation systems but Alberta Environment rejected it. They said they preferred to set up an internal working group so they could develop their own position. Here we are 89 years later and they don't even have a position!"

Although frustrated by the glacial speed of government response, Kerry Brewin is quick to add that the last decade has seen considerable improvement. "Ten years ago it was difficult even to get people to listen to you," he says. "There were few specific studies being done to evaluate fisheries issues at development sites along rivers. Those studies are being done now, and we're at the table more often than not."

Cliff Wallis, past president of the Friends of the Oldman River, wasn't at the Flowing to the Future conference. He was too busy trying to save the Oldman River from a dam many of the conference attendees were involved in building.

A decade later, Wallis feels guardedly optimistic about the future of Alberta's rivers. He believes that those who advise the Minister of Environment are giving him better advice. "The moral suasion of the advice given to the Minister is working," he says. "They're doing it, but they wouldn't put it in the Act for fear we would take them to court."

That's a legitimate fear. Since 1987, the Friends of the Oldman River have redefined the nature of environmental advocacy in Alberta by repeatedly challenging the provincial and federal governments in the courts. Led by the brilliant and uncompromising Cliff Wallis and Martha Kostuch, FOR initiated more than 10 major legal interventions in their battle to stop the Three Rivers Dam or, when it was already completed and filled, to have it decommissioned. Two cases went all the way to the Supreme Court. Canada owes its Canadian Environmental Assessment Act to FOR's successful battle to prove that the federal government had to obey its own environmental guidelines.

"We were treading water in 1989," said Cliff Wallis in an interview during the last weeks of the notorious Ty Lund's reign as Environment Minister. "The 1990s were a bad time for the environment but while we didn't make any gains, we at least held our ground. We've got some building blocks now, if we can get a good Minister and senior managers in Alberta Environment."

Among the new building blocks to which Wallis refers are Alberta's new Water Act, the Canadian Environmental Assessment Act (however, FOR and others have had to drag the federal government back into court to get it enforced), the Natural Resources Conservation Board (required to hold public hearings into major dams and diversions) and the reports and recommendations of the Northern River Basins Study.

The Athabasca, Peace, Slave and Lake Athabasca basins cover more than half the province. The Northern River Basins Study began in 1991 as a federal-provincial-territorial government response to public concerns about water pollution and watershed degradation by Alberta's new pulp mills and the Peace River's WAC Bennett Dam. The 24-member panel completed 150 technical reports and reviews, conducted public meetings and submitted its work to scientists across Canada for peer review.

In 1997 the governments of Canada, Alberta and N.W.T. formally responded to the panel's final report. The governments accepted all its recommendations, and then proceeded to explain how they would not implement them. The panel called for a pollution target of zero industrial discharge. The governments declared pollution prevention their first environmental priority, and then dismissed zero discharge as unworkable, opting instead for "best available technology"—in other words, the status quo. The panel called for the elimination of toxic substances. Governments agreed, and then argued that for several substances it couldn't be done and for the rest, they were already doing all they could.

The study flagged nutrient loading (overfertilizing rivers with sewage and pulp mill wastes) as a major problem. The panel called for nutrient discharges to be capped at 1996 levels, and then phased out. The governments offered to "strive" to reduce nutrients, and then explained why pulp mills need to continue dumping them. Alberta and Canada did agree to upgrade sewage treatment plants at Grande Prairie and Jasper. Work on the Grande Prairie facility began in 1998, while Jasper's project is still in the planning phase.

In response to the need for more and better monitoring data, the Alberta government promised only to study information collected by pulp mill companies. The governments did, however, commit to more studies. Most are behind schedule or have yet to begin, but pulp mills continue to discharge industrial wastes into the Peace, Wapiti, Athabasca and other northern rivers while clearcutting their upstream watersheds.

After spending 4 and a half years and more than $12 million on a comprehensive scientific analysis of the deteriorating state of northern rivers, governments promised all the improvements possible—except meaningful ones. The industrialization of northern rivers appears to be government policy. Clean water, edible fish and a healthy environment are okay too-so long as they don't get in the way of industry.

The Bow River laps as peacefully against its riprapped banks today as when I was growing up beside it. I no longer enjoy the happy illusion that the future well-being of my home river is assured. Not long ago, the natural forces at play in their watersheds—seasonal changes in rainfall, fire and grazing, dry cycles and wet cycles—controlled Alberta's rivers. Today's rivers are controlled not by nature but by human choices. We determine how much water they will contain, and when. We change their chemistry at the mouth of each storm sewer, pulp mill discharge pipe and sewage treatment plant. Our bulldozers and trackhoes hem them in, constraining their need to shift course. If Albertans are river people, our choices too rarely are river choices.

"If we're going to do right by our rivers, more people need to get involved," says Cliff Wallis. "Even if they write only one letter per year. We need church groups, community groups, everyone out there to discuss these things and get active."

Although formidable, the energies of Cliff Wallis, Stewart Rood, Kerry Brewin and the few others who work for river conservation during the lulls between public controversies are not enough to protect rivers against exploitation. During those quiet times, powerful vested interests like the Alberta Irrigation Projects Association and Alberta Forest Products Association continue to lobby governments to favour their special interests. Alberta's rivers are increasingly vulnerable.

Cliff Wallis refuses to be drawn into a discussion of whether there is any hope for Alberta's rivers. Hope, to him, is something people create. "I just put my head down and do what needs to be done," he says. "I get my energy not from hope but from the danger of the downside: how much there is to lose."

The rivers will continue to let us know how well we succeed—or fail.

Yesterday's Fishing Tomorrow

"In the larger lakes, such as Emerald Lake and Lake Louise, the evening catch is generally the largest and with fair luck and a coch-y-bonddhu, the angler may, in a couple of hours, land 10 or 12 pounds of trout to his rod. These lake trout run from three-quarters to eight pounds, and give splendid sport, while the trout in the streams weigh from one pound to five pounds and are particularly gamy to play...

In an hour, 13 trout varying from half a pound to two pounds lie in my creel."

Julie Henshaw, Canadian magazine
July 1906

A century ago, the rivers and lakes of Alberta's mountain national parks offered phenomenal fishing.

Wealthy Americans discovered the high trails and far places of the Canadian Rockies in the late 1880s, soon after Canadian Pacific Railways completed Canada's first transcontinental railroad. The new rail line brought tourists to Banff, Laggan (Lake Louise) and Field, where horse-drawn wagons waited to take them to new luxury hotels. The more adventurous hired outfitters for horseback camping expeditions into the wilderness beyond the Bow and Athabasca valleys.

Canada's federal government set aside Banff and Yoho national parks soon after the railroad arrived. Jasper became a park in 1906, a few years before rail lines penetrated the Yellowhead route. The government created those parks as instant tourist attractions to help the railroads attract customers to help pay down the immense debts they had run up building the lines. Although protecting scenery and wildlife was important, nobody was particularly worried about ecological integrity in those days-the whole country was wild, after all.

Besides mountain climbing and wildlife, the railroads touted the fishing in their new parks. And the fishing was great. Bull trout in many of the Rockies' glacier-fed lakes and rivers had lived 30 years without seeing a fisherman's shadow. Many weighed more than nine kilograms. During the fall spawning period, most of the biomass of whole streams could be locked up in several dozen huge char hugging the bottoms of a few deep pools.

An early Banff guide, Ralph Edwards, described an afternoon's fishing on the Bow River, halfway between Lake Louise and Bow Lake. At a big pool near camp, his American clients found a school of trout and soon grew frustrated by their stubborn refusal to take artificial flies, real flies, bacon or even mountain goat meat. Finally, just before they had to leave, one tried a spinner.

"Without any great enthusiasm the General made his cast, and the bait had barely touched the water when—zing—out went the line across the pool, with a leaping, fighting trout of considerable size at the end of it...As soon as he was landed and off the hook, out came the General's pocket scales and his prize was found to weigh five and half pounds...

"Now that they had discovered what the fish wanted, there was no lack of sport. First one speckled beauty and then another was hooked, played and finally landed. Several of the fish were really big fellows, some going eight and nine pounds. All small fish, that is, fish not weighing more than three or four pounds, were carefully returned to the water...We had 10 fish weighing 78.5 pounds, four of these exceeding nine pounds each."

Such fish are virtually unknown today. The bull trout, in fact, has been designated a threatened species over much of its range. Native cutthroat trout populations are so depleted that the Alberta and B.C. governments have joined the national parks in reducing catch limits to two or, in many streams, zero. Several spawning and rearing streams now are closed completely, so depleted are their native fish stocks.

Bull trout are fish of healthy, undisturbed watersheds. They grow slowly in mountain lakes and streams whose waters are too cold and changeable to support abundant algae and insects. Frontier bull trout grew huge because they lived so long and fed voraciously. They have little choice about their feeding habits considering that only big bull trout spawn successfully, and few mountain streams produce abundant food. I once caught a large bull trout that grabbed a small cutthroat I was playing and held on stubbornly until I had dragged him well up on the bank. Only then did he let go.

Such aggressive feeders were easy prey for fishermen. Many frontier-era photographs show proud anglers with strings of huge trout strung between trees. In those days it was a matter of pride to catch and kill as many trout as possible. Most of the victims rotted, were stolen by bears or got thrown away. Some people took pride in wiping out whole spawning runs of bull trout in only one or two seasons, often by dynamiting or snagging. Bull trout lie on the bottoms of pools when threatened by danger, rather than fleeing under banks like other fish, making them easy to poach.

Bull trout do not reach spawning age until they are 35 centimetres long. As a result, far more made it into frying pans than into spawning beds.

Westslope cutthroats—among the most beautiful trout in the world—inhabited many lakes and streams from the Bow River watershed south to the U.S. border. Cutthroats do not grow as big as bull trout, but there are more of them and they spawn at a smaller size. Although less readily fished out, they soon vanished from most accessible waters. So, too, did the unique little rainbow trout that were native to the Athabasca River's headwaters farther north.

Having promoted the fishing in the mountain parks, the railways soon faced the dilemma of rapidly deteriorating fisheries. The solution: stock more.

Nobody knows when tourism promoters stocked the first trout in Banff National Park, but it was almost certainly in the late 1800s. A brochure published in the first decade of the 20th century said: "Many of the mountain lakes are teeming with fish...All the best fishing lakes are being constantly restocked from the government hatchery at Banff, so that the fishing is growing better every year."

By the 1920s national park authorities had built fish hatcheries at Banff, Jasper and Waterton. Park wardens and fish hatchery staff poured millions of fish—none of them native to the Canadian Rockies-into just about every body of water that could wet a trout's dorsal fin. The rationale was simple: stock more fish and more people will catch fish; as word gets around, more people will come to the national parks and leave their money behind.

The huge bull trout, native westslope cutthroats and unique little Athabasca rainbows that had once given wilderness streams their unique character, gave way to Yellowstone and coastal cutthroats, Kamloops rainbow and eastern brook trout—not to mention Atlantic salmon, golden trout, ouaninache, Quebec red trout and arctic grayling. Besides stocking overfished water bodies, officials poured hatchery stock into lakes and streams that had never held fish before. If lakes were too small to sustain fish populations through the winter, wardens stocked them annually with catching-size fish.

By the 1950s and 60s, the mountain parks were again an angler's paradise. Fred Carter, who grew up in the Jasper area during that era, is still unhappy about the 1972 closure of the Jasper Fish Hatchery. "When I was a kid the fishing here was absolutely unbelievable," he says. "We used to head up to Caledonia Lake-you should have seen the brookies there used to be in there-or some of the other lakes around town, and they were all just full of fish."

Wardens stocked Patricia Lake as many as nine times a year in the 1960s. The Jasper hatchery had far more capacity than it needed, and the fish just kept pouring out. Wardens packed bags of trout into remote lakes. They poured thousands of Yellowstone cutthroats into hidden beaver ponds. For special occasions, the hatchery workers turned loose old brood rainbows—females weighing 3.5 or more kilograms-in small lakes near the hatchery.

All that stocking yielded good fishing—but it also devastated the natural ecosystems of the mountain parks. Fairy shrimp went extinct in some lakes. Food chains fell apart. Exotic bait fish took over lakes and wetlands. Exotic trout species outcompeted and hybridized with natives.

Bull trout vanished utterly from some lakes and streams.

The view from a national park roadside can be deceiving. Few visitors to the green and scenic mountain parks can see any evidence of the degree to which officials once manipulated seemingly pristine waters to produce trout. Many accessible lakes have weirs or other control structures to control water levels. Some have had streams diverted into them. Toxins from past deliberate poisonings continue to lurk in bottom sediments—and the bodies of fishes and other water creatures.

Banff's Vermilion Lakes may be Canada's most photographed and painted icon of mountain wilderness. They are, however, far from untrammelled. Tourism boosters stocked the lakes with exotic trout as early as the 1890s. Since anglers prefer not to be annoyed by mosquitos, they also released non-native mosquitofish to control the little bloodsuckers. Mosquitos still abound, but a unique species of fish—the Banff long-nosed dace—went extinct because of competition from the newcomers. In 1950, the Parks Service built a dam on Willow Creek to keep First Vermilion Lake full. In 1955 wardens poisoned the lakes with rotenone to kill off suckers and other native fish that, popular prejudice then believed, competed with trout for food. Wardens killed mink, kingfishers, otters and ospreys until the 1960s to protect the introduced fishes. In the early 1960s work crews even built artificial spawning beds for brook trout in First and Third lakes, then poisoned the lakes with herbicides to keep weed growth under control. In 1975, the dam on First Lake was upgraded. The scenic beauty of Banff's Vermilion Lakes conceals a disconcerting history of abuse.

But early fish culture efforts paid ecological dividends too. The Maligne River system, for example, had no fish until the late 1920s. For many years park wardens stocked brook trout in Medicine and Maligne lakes. Medicine Lake remained unproductive until the late 1960s, when wardens planted rainbow trout in it for the first time.

Today this unique fishery—which includes Maligne Lake, the largest glacier-fed lake in the Rockies, Medicine Lake, which virtually disappears each fall and Maligne River, one of the most beautiful whitewater rivers anywhere—has become renowned for its fishing. Anglers flock to Maligne Lake to troll for fat eastern brook trout and heavy-bodied rainbow trout. Others cast flies over schools of rainbows that cruise the shallows of Medicine Lake. It is not just human anglers who benefit from the exotic fish that now sustain their own populations by spawning. Harlequin ducks feed on trout eggs at the Maligne Lake outlet. Three pairs of ospreys and a pair of bald eagles nest in the valley. Kingfishers, mink and other animals that once had no reason for visiting the valley now call it home. Adding trout to the Maligne system produced enduring benefits for both anglers and native wildlife.

But by the time a virus infection forced the Parks Service to close down its Jasper hatchery in 1972, wardens and fisheries biologists had already begun to wonder if the stocking programs were worth the expense and trouble. The fishing was great, but especially in the shallow, formerly fishless ponds near Jasper, it wasn't natural. And in a lot of cases, the fishing was not what it should be. Most stocked fish never found their way into anglers' creels, making the expense of this kind of fish management hard to justify at a time of declining budgets.

Partly because of biological studies and partly in response to public demand that national parks be managed as natural ecosystems, the last decades of the 20th century saw the end of fish stocking in the national parks. At a 1989 national workshop on park fisheries management several people even called for the end of all fishing in national parks. Fishing, after all, is the only activity allowed in a national park that involves killing animals. Most park managers continue to value angling as a way for people to develop close, personal bonds with nature, as well as a management tool to keep numbers of non-native trout under control. Even so, the question won't go away. A panel of experts commissioned to look into the ecological health of Canada's national parks in 1999 stopped just short of calling for a ban on recreational angling.

Fish stocking may be finished in the national parks, but angling continues for now. Modern regulations no longer emphasize generous creel limits and long open seasons. Bull trout, in fact, now receive total protection. Banff prohibits anglers from killing cutthroat trout. Other parks restrict their take to two. In arguing for a reduced lake trout limit in the Lake Minnewanka reservoir and a similar restriction on cutthroats in Marvel Lake, former Chief Park Warden Perry Jacobson said: "In both of those lakes our creel censuses show that there is something stressing breeding-age adults; the big ones just aren't there for some reason."

Lake Minnewanka is a popular fishery, and commercial guides who profit from it resist regulation changes. But the very fact that anglers troll for lake trout in its deep waters points to the fact that not all the fishery problems in national parks originate with anglers and fisheries managers. Lake Minnewanka is an artificial reservoir that fills a once-wild valley that formerly contained three much smaller lakes.

The loss of mature lake trout from Minnewanka might be caused by TransAlta Utilities, which uses the reservoir to generate electric power. Water levels fluctuate three to six metres each year, at the worst possible times for the trout. Retired Parks Canada fisheries biologist Percy Wiebe points out that another power dam, on Spray Lakes, forever destroyed three different cutthroat fisheries in Banff's Spray River watershed. Where cutthroats to six kilograms used to be caught in the Spray, what little flow remains now produces only small brook trout and cutthroats.

Jasper's native Athabasca rainbow trout may be extirpated; a victim of past stocking programs that contaminated the gene pool. In Waterton, research suggests that native cutthroat trout may be gone forever, replaced by non-native strains. In all three parks, bull trout remain scarce. Percy Wiebe is not surprised that native trout—the ones that Julie Henshaw and Ralph Edwards fished for a century ago-are in trouble. "They've got to be endangered," he says. "We've done our very best to decimate them!"

The old days of trout-stocking, rotenone-poisoning and water-control dams are gone. Instead, national park managers today are trying to undo a century's worth of well-intentioned and naive ecological abuse. New regulations stress bait bans, closed seasons during spawning periods, protection for native species and an ongoing effort to focus angling kill on introduced, non-native species.

Perry Jacobson feels that most anglers are prepared to accept restrictive regulations if they understand the reasons behind them. "There really are very few real gluttons any more," he says. "People know that the resource can only benefit from being conservative. You're not going to hurt a resource by restricting it, but you can by exploiting it."

Anglers can still find excellent fishing in Canada's mountain national parks. But it isn't what the CPR described, and it will never again be what Fred Carter experienced in his boyhood. The future will see an increasing emphasis on protecting trout and other fish that are native to the mountain ecosystem, accompanied by much reduced kill limits.

Fishing in the Rocky Mountain national parks should be different from fishing elsewhere—because the national parks are different from other places. These are special places where, instead of consuming the natural world, we celebrate it and learn from it. Anglers—with or without more enlightened regulations—could choose to treat angling in parks as a form of nature study with a hook, rather than a way of getting a cheap meal. If so, the near future may hold schools of huge bull trout and lakes full of big native cutthroats such as were last seen more than a century ago, in that naive and hopeful frontier era that gave Canada her first national parks.

The Conservation Century

One day in Nova Scotia, T.R. Pattilo killed 16 ducks with four shots. This, by his standards, was great hunting. The trick was to blast them on the water while they were bunched tightly. Later, he boasted of dropping seven geese and wounding five others with only one shot. One of his best kills resulted from a midnight boat trip into the middle of a sleeping flock of blue-winged teal. He and his partner fired four shots that resulted in: "...dead ones by the dozen, very sick ones a great number, wing-broken ones not to be estimated, the whole making a great slaughter."

Pattilo was so delighted with the abundance of Canadian game that he published a book about it in 1902: Moose Hunting, Salmon Fishing and Other Sketches of Sport.

English sporting writer R.B. Marston, who wrote an introduction for Pattilo's book, dryly noted: "Our author certainly had grand sport, and although it cannot be so good as formerly, let us hope there is still game enough left to be worth going for."

There wasn't.

A century ago, Pattilo and his ilk wreaked havoc on Canada's wildlife populations. Commercial whalers and fur traders armed the north's indigenous people and paid them to slaughter muskoxen and caribou for the hide and meat trade. Fishermen along the St. Lawrence and the Atlantic coast robbed millions of eggs from gull and gannet colonies, shooting the adults by the thousands. In B.C., gunners killed brant and other waterfowl—both in spring and fall. Market hunters supplied growing towns and cities with deer, moose, bear and other wild meat.

Most people viewed Canada as an endless storehouse of fish, fowl, big game and other natural resources. If some thought game supplies couldn't last, they nevertheless felt plundering it made sense. Wildlife-rich wilderness would have to give way sooner or later to civilization, after all. Too bad the game couldn't last, but that's the price of progress.

In that environment, game hogs and slaughterers like Pattilo fit right in. Their greed merely hastened the inevitable. Canada's short history had already proved that the advance of civilization doomed even super-abundant species. Plains bison were extinct in the wild by 1885. No less abundant in eastern deciduous forests than the bison had been on the plains, passenger pigeons vanished forever by 1914. Pattilo, blasting bloody swaths through rafts of Atlantic waterfowl, never got a chance to sluice a Labrador duck or sea mink—they had already vanished into history.

Hunting north of Elko, B.C. in 1905, William T. Hornaday commented, "It was indeed a keen pleasure to see a living, wild, adult bull elk in British Columbia, and to know for fair that even there the species is not yet extinct." Even though there was a closed season on elk, Hornaday's hunting was not unduly constrained: his B.C. hunting licence entitled him to kill five male caribou, five goats, three rams, five deer, two bull moose. The 12 large animals he and his hunting partner eventually shot included two female grizzlies, six goats and four bighorn rams.

Salted hides and heads securely stowed (and with five baby mountain goats captured live for his zoo) Hornaday returned to New York to write, in all sincerity, "There is no such thing as safety for any wild creature, save under man's own laws."

At the beginning of the 20th century Canadians were, for the most part, aliens. Colonists spilled across the country, bent on changing it into something closer to their ideas of home-ideas imported from the domesticated landscapes of England and France. To these strangers, Canada's wilderness and wildlife had no value in their own right; they were merely resources to be exploited in the interests of development.

Not everyone felt this way, of course. Even during the pell-mell expansionism of the early 1900s, some argued for making fish, wildlife, timber and other resources last. Naturalists like Ernest Thompson Seton published books and articles criticizing the unregulated slaughter of frontier wildlife. As the century's first decade ended, Canadians began to hear from south of the 49th parallel about a new concept called "conservation."

Conservation was essentially an agricultural concept imported to North America from Europe by foresters like Gifford Pinchot. Promoters of conservation argued that natural resources like trees, trout and deer are crops that—with wise and prudent management—can sustain themselves indefinitely while humans crop the excess. At the dawn of the 21st century the idea seems almost elementary; in the early 1900s, however, it was radical.

American champions of conservation-people like Theodore Roosevelt, George Bird Grinnell and William Hornaday-were for the most part wealthy industrialists and influential members of eastern society. They organized clubs like the Audubon Society and the Boone and Crockett Society to lobby for stronger laws, better enforcement and wildlife sanctuaries where game could breed and increase. They also promoted more responsible behaviour by hunters.

Canada was a bureaucratic British colony rather than a freewheeling libertarian republic. Power in Canada was concentrated not in a capitalist elite but in the cold halls of government. Canada's most visionary early conservationists, consequently, were senior civil servants. Naturalists' clubs like the Ottawa Field-Naturalists and fish and game protective associations in the various provinces lobbied for better protection of wildlife, but it was the careful diplomatic manoeuvring of waistcoated bureaucrats that pulled Canada's wildlife back from the brink.

James Harkin, an unabashedly idealistic conservationist, became Canada's first Commissioner of National Parks in 1911. A career civil servant, he understood how the young country's political winds blew. Instead of arguing the intrinsic value of wilderness or the aesthetic value of wild animals, Harkin gathered facts and figures to show the economic value of national parks. When he showed politicians of the day that tourists were already bringing $50 million each year to the Rocky Mountains, and that tourism in the European Alps was worth three-quarters of a billion dollars each year, parliament's resistance to the idea of more national parks melted away.

Furbearing animals, big game and waterfowl never had to prove their economic worth, but other creatures did. In 1934, when Percy Taverner wrote the first Birds of Canada, he argued that: "Even the unsentimental, practical man, who has little outward sympathy with abstract beauty, has his attention attracted by the evident economic value of birds. Birds of Canada has been written to awaken and stimulate an interest, both aesthetic and practical, in the study of Canadian birds; to suggest the sentimental, scientific and economic value of that study...." To gain support for the 1917 Migratory Birds Convention Act and other early wildlife legislation, early Canadian conservationists like Taverner and Gordon Hewitt, of Canada's Department of Agriculture, relied heavily on arguments about the importance of songbirds in controlling agriculture pest insects. Wildlife had to pay its way before early Canadian society would bother protecting it.

Both the early conservation movement and the park preservation movement were founded in a similar belief in the incompatibility of human enterprise and nature. The only way to sustain wild things, this world view argued, was either to protect it carefully in parks, or to control and manage it under agricultural production models, while carefully regulating human "harvest" with game laws. Some of the earliest parks were meant to serve as breeding grounds for wildlife so that recovering populations could recolonize depleted areas nearby, restoring good hunting and trapping there. When James Harkin was trying to convince the government to establish a national park in northwestern Alberta, he insisted that, "These animals would soon learn that they were protected in this area and as they would breed there under the most favourable conditions the overflow should in a short time serve to supply a very large, contiguous district."

Although conservation in the early 20th century was mostly a practical matter of making supplies last, each passing decade increased the number of Canadians who identified personally with what were now their home landscapes. The generation whose tastes had been formed in overcivilized Europe gave way to new generations whose idea of home was shaped by Canadian wildness. Books like Taverner's Birds of Canada made it possible to identify and learn about native birds, rather than the nightingales, starlings and turtledoves in the European books most pioneers had brought with them. Ernest Thompson Seton wrote Wild Animals I Have Known and other nature stories that drew readers into a more sympathetic consideration of the plight of Canada's wildlife. The Group of Seven created art that validated the rugged beauty of Canada's wild places.

If wilderness and wildlife were part of how Canadians were coming to know themselves, then the devastation of songbirds, cranes, shorebirds and waterfowl took on an increasing urgency. Game protection associations sprang up all across Canada in the 1910s and 1920s in response to the need to lobby governments for better protection.

Partly because of the growing support from grassroots hunting groups, Canada and the U.S. achieved their biggest single conservation success with the signing of the Treaty for International Protection of Migratory Birds in 1916. Canada passed the Migratory Birds Convention Act in 1917 to ratify this unprecedented treaty that protected all waterfowl, shorebirds and songbirds. The Act gave the federal government jurisdiction over migratory birds, which had, until then, been considered the responsibility of provincial governments. To establish effective regulations, enforcement strategies and sanctuaries, the government established an Advisory Board on Wildlife Protection. The board included five powerful civil servants, all staunch defenders of wildlife: James Harkin, Gordon Hewitt of the federal Department of Agriculture, who had been Canada's point man in negotiating the treaty, James White of the Conservation Commission, Rudolph Anderson, a zoologist with the Canadian Geological Survey and Duncan Campbell Scott of the Department of Indian Affairs.

One of their first acts was to draft a law to protect muskoxen, caribou, arctic foxes and other northern wildlife from commercial slaughter. The law came just in time, as populations plummeted toward extinction. Like other measures to eliminate spring hunting, establish closed seasons and bag limits, and put wildlife sanctuaries in place, the Northwest Game Act and the Migratory Birds Convention Act focused mostly on reducing how many game animals hunters could kill. It made sense, given the unbelievable carnage that guns wreaked on wildlife in the late

1800s and early 1900s. Meanwhile, Canada was filling up with people. Wildlife habitat was disappearing-a far more serious threat.

The losses—especially where waterfowl habitat was concerned—became particularly obvious during the dirty thirties when drought magnified the already-severe impact of wetland drainage in the prairie provinces. Writing in 1934, Percy Taverner said "...the Migratory Birds Convention Act...has accomplished what could be expected of it and has staved off an evil day, but new factors have developed or have increased in importance. With a momentary increase of game more guns have been produced to kill and the killing has been better organized: more marshes have been drained and meadows trodden by cattle. Strange diseases have swept in epidemic through the feathered ranks and dry seasons have destroyed thousands. Lately comes news of the disappearance (perhaps permanently) of the eel grass of the Atlantic coast; the main food reliance of many winter geese...It is not desired to be pessimists or alarmists, but with these adverse factors appearing and no favourable ones adequate to the situation developing, the future of our waterfowl is far from hopeful."

Duck hunters in the United States became so concerned that, in 1937, they organized Ducks Unlimited and began to raise funds to buy, build or restore waterfowl habitat in western Canada. Quiet-spoken DU field staff like Alberta's George Freeman worked with farmers to promote land use practices that would produce crops without squandering ducklings. The time had come for citizen conservationists—mostly hunters—to shift conservation's focus from regulating the kill to restoring land health and protecting habitat. The 1930s saw a surge of grassroots activity that continued to grow right through the rest of the century. Groups like the Alberta Fish and Game Association and Ontario Federation of Hunters and Anglers organized sportsmen into powerful political lobby groups to push for better forestry practices, wilderness protection and habitat acquisition. Years later, U.S.-based groups like Trout Unlimited, the Nature Conservancy, the Rocky Mountain Elk Foundation and others would follow Ducks Unlimited's lead by expanding into Canada, bringing their fund-raising power to the challenge of making sure wildlife had places to live.

The ethic of fair chase hunting was firmly established by the 1950s and 1960s, and the role of the hunter-conservationist in lobbying for government regulation had paid off abundantly. White-tailed deer populations, once devastated from Manitoba through to the Maritimes, rebounded in response to closed seasons, conservative bag limits and the new ethic of responsible restraint on the part of hunters. Waterfowl darkened prairie skies again. Each fall's tally of migrating whooping cranes-whose numbers had sunk as low as 16 by mid-century-brought more hopeful news.

But the postwar years also brought an extended binge of resource development that cost wildlife more habitat than ever. As the wet 1950s gave way to drier conditions in the 1960s prairie duck populations began to fall again-this time because of lost breeding habitat, not overhunting. B.C. and Ontario promoted forestry development, beginning the process of overallocating wildlife habitat to increasingly mechanized logging companies. Simultaneously, responding to the demand for more energy to fuel all the economic growth, governments across Canada raced to dam rivers, flooding some of the country's most productive wildlife habitat. Alberta's oil industry ripped open once-pristine foothills and northern game ranges, cutting new roads that exposed once-isolated elk, moose and caribou herds to overhunting. Regulations that had worked when access was poor and habitat abundant, failed to protect game populations as industry and government opened up the hinterland.

Andy Russell gave up guiding hunters into the Alberta Rockies in the early 1960s, becoming one of many victims of development run amok. Horrified by the hasty destruction of so much that had once been wild and abundant he later wrote in Grizzly Country, "The grizzly was being no longer threatened...by unrestricted hunting. Now there was an even more frightening menace: that clanking, stinking, noisy invention of the devil known as a bulldozer." His experience with the ravages of what he now calls "multiple abuse" turned him from wilderness guide to conservation activist.

Andy Russell was not alone. In response to the postwar development orgy many new wilderness conservation organizations arose-from the National and Provincial Parks Association of Canada (now the Canadian Parks and Wilderness Society) to the Alberta Wilderness Association and Canadian Nature Federation. No longer was it just hunters setting Canada's conservation agenda—now a broader cross-section of society was taking responsibility.

The 1970s saw a further proliferation of grassroots groups defending nature against pesticide abuse, industrial pollution, commercial exploitation of national parks and other threats to wildlife and wild places. Canada's consciousness of its stewardship responsibilities came of age in the 1970s and 1980s as an increasingly educated and increasingly native-born population looked at the consequences of decades of feverish development and growth and began to realize what they stood to lose.

But if growing numbers of Canadians were finally arriving home as citizens of a land that has always been defined by its wildness and wildlife, politicians were turning down other roads. The neoconservative political mood of the 1980s and 1990s brought a new set of conservation challenges that looked, to those with a sense of history, all too familiar. Where visionary public servants once fought to close off commercial markets for dead animals, a new generation of calculator-brained bureaucrats opened up new markets in the 1980s. One province after another legalized commercial farming of native elk and deer. By the late 1990s, starting in Saskatchewan, they began to allow game ranchers to charge "hunters" for the right to shoot captive-raised animals in enclosures. Those who forget history are doomed, it would appear, to repeat it. Game farms fence wild animals out of habitat previously available to them. Diseases like tuberculosis and mad deer disease fester inside. And as captive herds proliferate, wildness ceases to be a valued attribute of animals previous generations fought to restore.

Where early fish and game clubs fought to ban spring hunting, baiting and game hogs, by the end of the twentieth century some were fighting to defend killing of bears—and even deer—over bait. Fair chase arguments gave way to rants against gun control, off-road vehicle restrictions and animal rights groups. The hunter-conservationist tradition that had emerged out of a murky, shallow sea of self-interest began to sink back into it. Game-hog Pattilo might have recognized some kindred spirits; Roosevelt and Harkin likely would have shaken their heads in disgust.

In spite of setbacks and new problems, however, Canada is in many ways a richer and more hopeful place at the beginning of the 21st century than at the start of the 20th. Many endangered species like whooping cranes, trumpeter swans and white pelicans are far better off today than they were back when Pattilo and his brethren were flock-shooting waterfowl into near oblivion. Canada has far more national parks, ecological reserves and wilderness areas than it did then. White-tailed deer may be more abundant now than at any time in history. Elk have returned to Ontario. Muskoxen and caribou thrive in the north. Geese, if anything, are too abundant. Even wolves, animals with which humans have always had the most ambivalent of relationships, are more widely distributed and popular today than they were in much of the last century.

Still, Canada's wild spaces continue to shrink, while our population and its appetites grow. Immense challenges face us in the new millennium. We have little time left to come to terms with the hard fact that both human ambition and ecological resilience have limits-limits that may shrink in response to a volatile, changing climate. By themselves, 20th century models of conservation will likely prove insufficient for the coming challenges. Even so, 20th century Canadian conservationists like Ernest Thompson Seton, James Harkin, Percy Taverner, George Freeman, Andy Russell and countless others will always serve as examples of the passion and perseverance that successful conservation demands. A century of conservation achievements stand as proof of what a few individuals with determination and vision can achieve.

In a 1915 speech to the Canadian Conservation Commission, Gordon Hewitt declared that future generations of Canadians "...would blame us if they found out we had allowed this fauna to become extinct and to disappear forever when it was in our power to preserve it."

Hewitt died five years later, one of the great conservationists of

Canadian history. Reflecting on his achievements, William Hornaday said, "May heaven send to wildlife more men like him." Heaven did. Canada has been abundantly blessed as a result.

Now it's our time to honour that legacy as we confront the conservation challenges of a new century. May we prove no less worthy than those before us who served Canada's wildlife and wild places so well.

Things with Sharp Teeth

Real Grizzlies; Real People

"If you meet a strange trapper and desire to take a measure of his moral leanings," wrote William Hornaday in his 1906 hunting classic Campfires in the Canadian Rockies, "Ask his opinion of the moral character and mental capacity of the wolverine. I have heard trappers solemnly declare that no matter how much any one may malign this particular devil, its character is much blacker than it can be painted."

Hornaday and his companions hunted the headwaters of British Columbia's Elk and Bull rivers, where wolverines—despite their sordid reputation—survive to this day.

During his travels, Hornaday saw no wolverines and glimpsed only a few grizzly bears. He was less than impressed by the bears. "Fifty years ago the grizzly bear was an animal which knew not fear of any living thing; and then he was Great. Today the grizzly is a quitter. In nine cases out of every 10, the moment he sees a man, he runs from him, frantically."

How we view—and treat—our fellow creatures tells more about us than about them. In this regard, William Hornaday's observation about trappers and wolverines was right on the money. He did not, however, seem to recognize that his own impression of the grizzly was every bit as telling.

Hornaday, like Theodore Roosevelt, George Bird Grinnell and other wealthy easterners of the day, saw western hunting as a frontier pastime, coloured by myth and inevitably doomed by the onrush of civilization. The great grizzlies William Hornaday longed to meet were the ferocious man-killers Lewis and Clark—having seen bears through their own set of biases and generally having shot and wounded them at first sight—reported along the Missouri River a century earlier. Hornaday, nostalgic for the passing of the frontier, was sure that bears were already something less than what they had once been.

Hornaday, like most of us, never really knew the grizzly. He knew, and hunted, its myth—a savage creature, more powerful and dangerous than the men who hunted it, defending its doomed wilderness against the manifest destiny that must inevitably put all of North America's landscapes into the useful service of humanity. Hornaday's party killed two grizzlies on his trip to the Canadian Rockies but they were disappointing bears—not nearly fierce enough to satisfy his fantasies.

Hornaday was wrong about the inevitable loss of hunting. Hunting is better in the Bull and Elk River valleys now than in his time, when elk had been hunted into near oblivion. Grizzly bears still thrive there too, in spite of frontier myths and human fears. And Hornaday would still be disappointed with them because they are not the savage and heroic giants he believed grizzlies should be. They are, and always were, simply bears.

When I hunt Hornaday's country today, I know I might meet a grizzly. I also know that the world has changed for the great bear, and his future is far from assured. Hornaday hoped to shoot a grizzly. I hope never to. Hornaday considered the grizzly doomed to ultimate extinction. Like many other hunters still blessed with the opportunity to hunt real grizzly country, I am determined to prove him wrong. I stay constantly alert, approach downed game from upwind and carry a can of pepper spray on the strap of my pack where I can reach it quickly. It's more than common sense: it's a responsibility I owe the grizzly for the privilege of hunting in his domain.

Writing of the last grizzly killed in Arizona's White Mountains, Aldo Leopold said, "...it must be poor life that achieves freedom from fear." Hunting elk in grizzly country is not poor life; it is rich beyond measure—real hunting in real country. A mountain without grizzly tracks, on the other hand, has a hole in its heart. There is a vitality missing from the mountain, its elk and, ultimately, its hunters.

But the myth of the savage grizzly lives on, and the fear it breeds in the minds of many continues to work against the grizzly. People don't like feeling vulnerable, especially to other animals. Just as a bear's fear motivates most grizzly attacks, human fear conspires against the future of the bear.

Several years ago, a mother grizzly attacked and severely mauled my sister and her husband. Their injuries profoundly disturbed the attending physician. My sister continues to suffer to this day, and the physician continues to argue that Canada's national parks should be cleared of grizzlies to make them safe for people. No doubt he has treated similar or worse injuries resulting from automobile accidents, falls down mountainsides and drunken assaults. But my sister's injuries were from a wild animal. To those who share the doctor's values, this makes the injuries and their impacts not just horrifying, but morally offensive. Why should humans have to tolerate animals that behave like this?

The attack was, however, wholly natural and predictable. The mother grizzly was a small bear with young cubs. She had taken possession of a bighorn carcass beside a popular hiking trail. Being small, she probably felt more threatened by approaching humans than if she had been a larger, dominant animal. Female grizzlies become aggressive when they feel their young are in danger and—obliged to accumulate a quarter of their body weight as fat each year to survive the long winter sleep—most bears will defend a valuable food source aggressively. My sister and her husband walked right into her in a snowstorm. Nothing about the ensuing attack embittered or, in retrospect, surprised them, even though the resulting injuries changed their lives forever. Unlike the doctor who tended to them, they saw the grizzly for what it was and their accident for what it also was—the kind of purely rotten luck that sometimes happens to good people.

They, I believe, are closer to truly belonging to this place than that doctor—because they accept the Rockies as a place that comes with grizzlies and the uncertain risk of meeting them.

A decade after their injury, only a few kilometres away, I met another grizzly mother with her cubs. It was a bright June morning and I was checking to see if a secret beaver pond still held trout. The smell of mint surrounded me as I picked my way through a dew-covered meadow. Trampled swaths in the sedges showed where some large animals had wandered along the edge of the meadow. It occurred to me that bears might have been here earlier, but my mind was on other things.

Seeing no fish, I started back to the road. Just as I stepped into the aspens I saw crushed vegetation and smelled wet fur. I stopped. Something crunched a few feet away. It was a grizzly cub, rooting about in sweet cicely and cow parsnip. Another movement: another cub. Then I saw the mother, deeper into the shadows, her back and hump rippling as she fed.

A song sparrow sang behind me, out in the sunshine. He was oblivious to what was happening inside the forest fringe—it was just a bright June day and would continue to be one if, as I suddenly realized could happen, I were to die in the next few moments. Just another life-and-death encounter in the woods. My family and unfinished plans suddenly meant nothing; I was just a transient thing of living protein, utterly vulnerable.

The mother grizzly raised her head. Part of a cow parsnip stem hung from one side of her mouth as she stared at me, abruptly aware that she and her cubs were not alone. Her eyes were small, her nose wet. I could hear the pounding of my heart in my temples as I noted, out of the corners of my eyes, that the trees here were too small to climb.

Then she lowered her head, pulled up another mouthful of greenery and turned her back on me. She had chosen to give me space. I turned, legs still rubbery with adrenaline shock, and eased my way back out into the sunlight.

Hornaday would probably have shaken his head in disgust-what kind of grizzly was that?

It was a real grizzly—not a stereotype built around human fears. Over the years I've met several real grizzlies, at ranges as close as five metres. Any could have killed me, but each chose not to. On those occasions when I was armed, I made the same choice.

Fear, prejudice, human ignorance, macho fantasy and sheer greed—not the nature of the grizzly bear itself—account for the fact that grizzlies no longer survive in most of their historical range. We could live with grizzly bears if we were prepared to know them for what they are, not what we imagine them to be, and to adjust our own behaviour accordingly. The failings, where bears and humans overlap, are almost always human failings. Of the two species, after all, we are the one that boasts of our ability to learn, adapt, imagine and anticipate. And that is all we need to live safely with the bear. The absence of grizzly bears in most of the west reflects not only the loss of one of nature's crowning achievements, but a failure of humans to become truly human—to be all we are capable of being.

Grizzlies are intelligent animals that learn through experience. In crowded national parks like Yellowstone, Glacier, Waterton Lakes and Banff, many grizzlies learn to avoid human crowds by foraging only a few metres off the trails, out of sight of passing people. Where ranchers raise cattle in grizzly country, some bears learn to seek out calving areas to feed on stillbirths. Sometimes scavenging bears, having been exposed to the calving herds, learn to hunt live cattle. Others find garbage or stored livestock feeds and, once they've learned about the new way of getting high quality food, find it difficult to forget.

Where hunters return each fall to grizzly country, some bears learn to associate the influx of humans and the sound of gunshots with the onset of gut pile season. Hunters can learn too—most do—and hunting becomes a richer, more uncertain experience for the presence of hungry bears only too ready to take over a freshly killed elk carcass.

It's hard for a grizzly bear to do any differently. When humans and grizzlies interact, the only one with a lot of choice is the human. We are the ones who can choose to store garbage securely, haul calf carcasses away from calving pastures, carry bear spray and hunt with our minds alert to the possibility of a grizzly encounter. After a century of research and practical experience, there really isn't a lot left to learn about behaving sensibly around grizzlies. When we fail to make the right choices, however, the grizzly bear acts predictably and the depth, or shallowness, of our values determines how we interpret and respond to its behaviour. The combination of poor human choices and human-centred values has left a lot of grizzly country devoid of grizzlies.

The survival of the grizzly is the survival of wholeness and of wildness—not just in the landscape but also in ourselves. Grizzly tracks in the river mud, berry-filled scats on the trail, the sudden eruption of a startled silvertip out of the willows: those are among the things that make country most whole, and humans most real. Shooting an elk on a mountain is just that, unless there is a possibility of a grizzly there too. That is another thing altogether, a far richer thing.

If anyone should be promoting the continued well-being of the grizzly, and its restoration to the west's quiet places, it should be hunters. Who else, after all, knows and values the wild as intensely? Western hunters, in too many once-great places, have had to make do with Aldo Leopold's "poor life" for too long.

Ecologically, nothing really stands in the way of the grizzly returning to places from which human prejudice has banished it. Glacier lilies flower and wilt, uneaten, in the high Uintah Mountains. The spring-green foliage along streams that drain from Colorado's San Juan Mountains still hides elk calves each spring from grizzlies that are no longer there to hunt them. The tufted hairgrass in northern Idaho's timberline meadows is no less succulent than it was back when grizzly bears still grazed it a century ago. The saskatoons still ripen each August along the Milk River breaks. It's all still grizzly country—the only thing missing is the great bear itself.

Each fall, hunters return to those once-wild places. They see no grizzly tracks in the mud. There is no edge to their awareness as they stalk through the dark timber. They do the best they can; but without the great bear, their hunts, and the land they hunt, will be less than complete.

The grizzly is not Hornaday's savage frontier beast, nor an exciting diversion to entertain us in national parks, nor the devil's own beast who prowls the dark timber looking for a chance to murder human beings. It is simply itself: an animal that belongs in, and in many ways personifies, the west's wild places. When we allow human fear or arrogance to exclude it, we betray a smallness of spirit that lessens us.

"Relegating grizzlies to Alaska," Aldo Leopold wrote half a century ago, "is about like relegating happiness to heaven; one may never get there."

Learning to live with an animal that doesn't always share our own belief in human superiority, from this perspective, might be seen as a kind of work of salvation—both of the west's living places, and of we who like to think of ourselves as native to, and worthy of, those places.

The Grizzly Hunting Placebo

It was probably Bertha I met on the Lineham Trail one summer day in 1994. She was old even then. Her belly sagged and her jowls flapped as she moseyed up the trail, head down, toward me and my hiking companions.

We raised our arms and shouted to get the grizzly's attention. Thirty metres away she finally stopped and looked at us. She showed no surprise or aggression; if anything, she looked exasperated.

After assessing the situation, the old bear stepped off the trail and quietly picked her way through the deadfall, passing only 10 metres away. She vanished around a corner and climbed back onto the trail-right into the midst of a cluster of little girls and their camp counsellors. The quiet summer afternoon erupted into a chorus of terrified shrieks. By the time I ran up the trail to help, the bear, no doubt a nervous wreck by now, had vanished. The counsellors got the girls under control and they all hiked down the trail, wide-eyed with excitement.

We all expected the worst from that bear. But all she wanted was to go up a valley too full of humans. We were the problem, not her; she solved it peacefully in spite of our fear.

The grizzly's neutral acceptance of humans, and her age, led me to conclude that this bear might be Bertha. Bertha was one of the first bears biologist David Hamer radio-collared during a 1970s research study. Throughout the study she treated humans as little more than scenery. Her personality couldn't have been better suited to a grizzly bear living in a crowded national park.

Bertha, however, didn't spend all her time in a national park. Like most grizzlies, her home range was larger than the tiny 525-square-kilometre Waterton National Park. In early 1997 a hunter shot her as she wandered through the ranching country north of the park looking for cow afterbirths and new greenery. She was at least 26 years old.

The media took quite an interest in Bertha's death. The debate over whether Alberta should continue to allow grizzly hunting was raging loudly in Calgary and Edmonton. Since Bertha had a name and a history her passing somehow seemed particularly poignant.

Biologically, however, Bertha's work was done. The elderly bear could no longer produce offspring. Her teeth were so loose that one virtually fell out in the hand of a wildlife officer examining her carcass. Bertha had been due to die.

Most game biologists estimate that grizzly populations can sustain a loss of maybe four to five percent each year to all forms of human-caused mortality, including hunting. If 20 grizzlies range south of Pincher Creek (Alberta Environment estimates 35 or so), and hunting is the only unnatural source of losses, then the population could withstand Bertha's loss. Nobody, however, knows how many grizzlies live in the area.

Until somebody figures out how to count bears, however, the argument about whether hunting is a threat to grizzly numbers will not end. With the advent of new methods of genetic fingerprinting, that may be happening. In the late 1990s biologists from B.C., Alberta and Parks Canada began testing new methods of inventorying grizzly bears with scent-bait stations. When grizzlies investigate the foul-smelling baits, they leave tufts of hair on strands of barbed wire strung around the bait. Biologists use the genetic material in each hair sample to identify individual bears. By repeatedly sampling the same area, biologists compare the number of bears whose hair they find more than once with the number of new bears that turn up each sampling period, to develop a statistical model of the bear population. Their final estimate was about 40 grizzly bears south of the Crowsnest Pass and 20 to 30 north of it.

Even with improved methods of estimating bear population numbers, provincial biologists try to take a biologically cautious approach to grizzly hunting. They estimate bear populations conservatively, and then set quotas on how many bears humans can kill or remove each year, again conservatively. If wildlife officers haul away any grizzlies to protect livestock and property, they subtract those from the number available to hunters. And, to protect breeding females, they forbid hunters to shoot females accompanied by cubs.

Bertha died in 1997. In 1996, a hunter shot a large male on a nearby ranch. Those were the only legal hunting kills south of Pincher Creek during that period. However, wildlife officers trapped and removed at least six other grizzlies in 1996, and at least 12 in 1997. Those bears had been attracted to poorly stored grain, the rotting carcasses of calves that died naturally and, in a few cases, the opportunity to hunt and kill domestic cattle. At least two were mature females. Not only did the population lose those bears; it lost all the cubs they might have produced. For an animal that produces so few young anyway, that's a big loss.

Hunters, in other words, had little impact on the area's grizzly population. Agricultural practices and "problem wildlife" policy had a far greater impact.

Ironically, grizzlies suffer even worse when ranching surrenders to other land uses. In the foothills around Okotoks or Cochrane, rural residential developments and small acreages have replaced the big ranches where grizzlies used to range. Grizzlies can't stay out of trouble when people proliferate across the landscape. That's why those areas no longer have any grizzlies at all. When ranchers sell out to developers, grizzlies lose habitat permanently.

Most ranchers in grizzly country never have any problems with grizzlies because they don't invite trouble. They clean up the carcasses of stillborn calves and other animals that die on the range, store their garbage and feeds safely, and know where bears are likely to be and how to avoid them. "It's always the same guys who have bear troubles," one rancher said to me. "Sort of tells you something, doesn't it?"

Alberta's foothills ranching country still has the potential to sustain good grizzly numbers, partly due to the continued survival of large ranches and the good stewardship of many ranchers. For that reason, educating and motivating the rest of the ranching community to adopt more bear-friendly management practices may do more for grizzlies in the long run than banning the spring grizzly hunt.

Whether to allow grizzly hunting is partly a biological question, partly a moral question and partly a socio-political question.

Biologically, grizzlies are among the slowest-reproducing animals in North America—probably because other animals rarely hunt them. They lack the biological characteristics of a prey species: high breeding rate, ability to quickly disperse and recolonize new ranges and high population densities.

Even so, the deaths of a few male bears may not hurt the population—if there are enough bears and their death rate from other causes is low enough. If biologists know how many grizzlies are in a population, how fast they reproduce and how many die of all causes each year, they can judge if it is safe to sell any grizzly hunting licences. Until they know that, the biologically sensible thing is to err on the side of caution and sell few or—as many now argue—none at all.

Morally, it's hard to justify shooting an animal you do not intend to eat, which has done you no harm and that the population may not be able to spare. But in a pluralistic society based on principles of freedom, most moral choices are generally left to the individual. As a hunter, I must constantly make moral decisions. Personally, I believe that killing a grizzly would be morally wrong; I never will. Others who work as hard as me for the conservation of bears and their habitat see things differently. For that reason, it seems risky to make grizzly hunting policy on the basis of any one group's moral position.

The socio-political side of the question is perhaps the most challenging. If government bans grizzly hunting, what will this say to rural residents who feel that the current hunting season keeps bears wild and controls their populations? That society as a whole has no interest in managing grizzlies, even though ranchers and other rural residents must continue to live with the bears and their potential dangers? If that is the nonverbal message, how many grizzlies will quietly—and illegally—vanish from isolated pastures as individuals take matters into their own hands? "Shoot, shovel, shut up" say the bumper stickers in Montana, where the U.S. Endangered Species Act rigorously protects grizzly bears. Some biologists speculate that closing the grizzly season in southern Alberta could result in the undocumented and illegal deaths of more bears than would be saved from hunters' bullets. Nobody, of course, really knows.

In the ongoing debate over how to conserve wildlife, hunting has always been an easy target. Those who hunt are a small minority in society. People who don't hunt can find it hard to believe that anyone who consciously chooses to kill animals honestly cares about wildlife. If you ban hunting, the simple logic goes, you save animals. That's what we want to do, right?

But dying is part of nature. In any population of wild animals, it isn't whether animals die that matters, it's how many and by what causes. Right now, in southern Alberta, more grizzlies die because of illegal kills, road kills and control removals, than from legal hunting. Limiting any of the former will accomplish far more than banning the latter.

In any case, what matters most to a grizzly is whether there is habitat worth living in, not how it will eventually die. The odds of postponing its inevitable death increase in direct proportion to the quality of habitat: roadlessness, wildness, naturalness. As another bumper sticker declares: "It's the habitat, stupid!"

Grizzlies are safest in wilderness. We need more of it. In fact, we need to think seriously about taking some habitat back from industry and restoring it to wildness. But grizzlies can also live, albeit less securely, in areas used for ranching and logging. The key is for responsible humans to make the right choices: remove garbage, clean up livestock carcasses, close roads and keep grizzlies from coming into conflict with people. We need to focus a lot more effort on this part of the conservation equation.

Grizzlies have never persisted long in a landscape fragmented by human development: this is why they no longer live near Okotoks, Cochrane or Great Falls, and are rare now even in Banff. Ultimately, the incremental subdivision of the rural west is the biggest threat to grizzlies and other wildlife. The energy used in the fight to ban grizzly hunting would be much more usefully spent on the far more difficult challenge of keeping human populations and human use as low as possible in bear country.

In any event, a decision to ban grizzly hunting will unquestionably work against the survival of the great bear if it becomes a sort of environmental placebo. It simply is not true that if hunters can't kill grizzlies, the bears will be safe. The real grizzly conservation priorities are far more complicated than simply locking up hunters' guns. The most important work must involve protecting scenic public lands from real estate promoters, stopping the insidious conversion of ranching country into increasingly cluttered complexes of acreages and rural residences, making ranching more bear-friendly, and keeping roads and industry out of our last wild places.

Wolves and the Wilds We Hunt

It was barely past noon, but the day was already fading fast toward dusk. In January the headwaters of the Athabasca River are a cold and silent place where the sun rarely shows itself above the peaks. Far below, the braided channel of the Athabasca was frozen and still. Weathered spars in icy ranks spread along the slope in all directions, the remains of a forest that had burned 10 years earlier. The snow was untracked. Nothing stirred.

The absolute, icy stillness of a mountain winter is something that permeates to your very core. To be alive in a landscape of grey rock, silent trees and snow, where the very air is frozen, is a strange and humbling sensation. So far as I could see I was the only living creature in the entire valley.

An hour later, after a treacherous ski down through the burn, I slid out onto the wind-hardened snow of the floodplain. There were still 10 kilometres between the cabin where I planned to spend the night and me. I set off downriver, skis hissing in the crusted snow. It was almost 40 degrees below freezing.

A tree cracked somewhere back in the forest. It was the first sound I had heard all day that I hadn't made myself.

At length I came to a place where the river had boiled up over its ice, spreading a thick blue sheet across my path. I left the channel and picked my way along the edge of a dwarf birch meadow.

Something flickered beyond the trees. I stopped, wondering if my eyes were playing tricks on me. Another slash of movement, and then a black wolf trotted into view, half a kilometre downstream. It was travelling upstream toward me.

I hunkered down in the lee of some driftwood, the cold forgotten.

Another wolf appeared, then two more. In single file they trotted along the edge of the floodplain.

About 100 metres away the big black paused, then turned and

crossed the flats obliquely below a patch of dark open water. The grey followed, then the two smaller blacks that had paused to investigate some odour also dashed across. The four wolves paused directly across the river from me. They sniffed noses, tails wagging. After a few moments the black turned and walked into the timber. The grey followed a moment later.

Left on their own, the smaller wolves sat on their haunches for a few minutes, and then continued up the river to a steep, willow-covered avalanche fan that spilled onto the floodplain. One cut up into the willows, and the other proceeded 100 metres upstream, then lay down in the open.

Far up the slope I saw the black wolf break out onto the avalanche slope, pause, and then cross slowly into the timber opposite. Below him, the grey appeared next, flushing two ptarmigan, which, like ghosts, coasted down the slide path and across the river, passing so close I could hear the hiss of frozen air in their wings.

A long while later, the black emerged from the timber far up the river. One by one the other wolves joined him and, single-file, they continued up the valley and disappeared around the next bend.

The valley was empty once more.

I felt like I was waking from a dream.

During the years that I studied wildlife in the Canadian Rockies, I ran into wolves on many occasions. Few encounters, however, have stayed with me so vividly as the day I watched those four wolves plan and execute an unsuccessful hunt on the headwaters of the Athabasca River.

Later that same winter I had another strange experience with a wolf on my way home to Jasper after an extended backcountry trip. Rounding a corner on Highway 93A, I saw a large white animal just slipping off the road. Figuring it must be a mountain goat, and wondering what it was doing so far from the nearest mountainside, I sped up, turned off the engine and coasted to a silent stop where the animal had disappeared.

Twenty metres away a huge white wolf stood motionless, staring back over his shoulder. He turned and began to lope up the bank into the pine forest.

Rolling down my window I stuck my face out and howled, hoping he would pause and give me another look at him. Instead, he turned, sat down and howled back. I howled again. So did he.

For five minutes we howled back and forth. The old wolf knew whom he was howling at; he was staring right at me. For some strange reason he seemed to want a conversation. At length he stood, shook himself and disappeared into the pines. I drove home, tingling with that strange sense of privilege that you sometimes get when a wild animal accepts you briefly into its own world.

One wolf can change your whole year. In that sense there is something about the wolf that other animals lack. We react more intensely to wolves than we do to moose, bear and deer. There is something about the wolf that reaches deep inside the human psyche and pulls out strong, often indecipherable, emotions.

You don't even have to see or hear a wolf to be affected by it; wolves seem to have as much impact in the abstract. Wolves have been extinct for decades in the lower 48 United States. Yet thousands of Americans who have never seen a wolf, have no reason ever to expect to see one, and who really don't know very much about them, have become impassioned defenders of wolves. No conservation program in the history of the United States of America was more wildly popular than the reintroduction of wolves into Yellowstone National Park and the wilderness areas of northern Idaho. Biologists wanted to restore a key predator to incomplete ecosystems. But the passion with which the American public in places as far away as Los Angeles and Manhattan latched onto the idea had more to do with the emotional appeal of the wolf than with ecosystem integrity.

Equally as intense is the reaction of many hunters who have never seen or heard a wolf. Normally civilized individuals nearly foam at the mouth at the thought of wolves eating elk calves and moose. In the early 1990s the Alberta Fish and Game Association started a predator control fund designed to reduce the number of wolves in parts of western Alberta. The organization raised more than $15,000 in less than a year. The money went to subsidize registered trappers who would otherwise not have trapped wolves since their pelts had little value.

Lyle Fullerton, former executive-director of the AFGA, said that the predator control fund was the most successful fund-raising effort the group has ever launched. "We received as much mail supporting the program as against it," he said. "But the difference was that the support mostly came from Alberta, while a lot of the letters against it came from various places in the United States."

The Alberta government officially frowned on the AFGA's short-lived venture into wolf management, but some predator biologists with Alberta Fish and Wildlife were privately glad to see it. When the province released a recovery plan in 1986 for the endangered woodland caribou, there was a great public outcry because the plan included a three-year program to reduce the number of wolves in key caribou areas. As a result, nervous politicians scuttled the caribou recovery plan in its entirety. The AFGA program arose in large part because of hunter frustration with government inaction.

For many years I hunted one of the target areas for that wolf control program. Other hunters told me that the place was overrun with wolves and big game was being wiped out. I saw wolf sign too; but each winter my freezer ended up full of elk and deer meat. It seemed to me then, and it seems to me now, that too many unsuccessful hunters prefer to blame anything and anyone but themselves. By the same token, it occurred to me that the wolves hunted the area for the same reason I did; it is full of game.

Nonetheless, John Gunson of the Alberta Fish and Wildlife Division has produced convincing evidence that wolf predation helped depress elk numbers in parts of the Brazeau River drainage. Gunson says that habitat change is the longer-term problem—what were once grassy meadows are now tangles of unpalatable swamp birch while old burns have filled in and become dense forest—but wolf predation in the reduced available elk habitat kills more elk calves than the population can spare.

Jan Edmonds, a caribou specialist with the division's Edson office, still believes that wolf numbers should be reduced to protect dwindling caribou herds in the northern foothills. Again, the critical problems are past overhunting, ongoing road kills and massive habitat loss to the pulp and paper industry. But north of Hinton where populations of moose, elk and deer, which thrive on second-growth that comes up after logging, sustain high numbers of wolves, caribou have fallen into a so-called "predator pit." Caribou are easier prey than moose or deer, so wolves tend to kill them opportunistically. The Catch-22, however, is that if the government temporarily reduces wolf numbers as Edmonds proposes, other prey species will likely increase. Once the wolf kill ends, wolves would then increase to even greater densities than now.

In any case, wolves are no longer the most pressing problem facing Alberta's caribou. In the early 1990s the Alberta government signed over all the critical caribou habitat in Edmonds' study area to logging companies. The old forests that caribous depend on are destined to become paper and, once the logged areas are replanted, the new forests will never be allowed to become old again. Wildlife populations can and do recover from heavy predation, but habitat loss is forever.

Indeed, many of the problems for which wolves get the blame can be traced to other causes. The dynamics of game populations, habitat, predators and human development are complex and interconnected. Many once-great elk ranges no longer support as many elk as they used to not because of wolves, but because the grassy, productive burned habitats that predominated in the early 20th century have given away to dense pine forest. A government-financed golf course and hotel complex stand on one of the most important elk winter ranges in Alberta's Kananaskis Valley. Across the continental divide in southeastern B.C.-once described as the Serengeti of North America-elk populations have crashed because of deliberate overallocation of hunting licences to reduce the number of elk competing with domestic cattle for pasture.

When game numbers begin to decline some hunters begin to look for easy scapegoats. In too many cases, wolves get the blame for problems actually caused by rotten habitat management, poor land use planning or failures in game management.

Fullerton, unlike some of the more outspoken members of the

AFGA, does not call for wolves to be exterminated. Nonetheless, he insists, in some places where wildlife populations are under stress for whatever reason, it might make sense to manage wolves as well as their prey. The AFGA, he says, is not interested in killing wolves off; what they want to do is to keep wolf numbers in balance with the needs of both game animals and human hunters.

If the government lacks the political will to manage wolves, some hunting groups seem to be saying that they will do it instead. But Dick Dekker, a tall, quiet-spoken biologist who has spent most of a lifetime tracking wolves and other wildlife in western Canada, argues that the AFGA is howling up the wrong tree.

"Why does the proposed remedy always centre on the natural predator?" asks Dekker. "What our wildlife needs is protection from people. Just look at the abundance of elk as well as wolves in Jasper Park. One February I was observing a wolf pack asleep on the frozen Athabasca River, while 18 elk, all six-point bulls, were grazing on nearby flats. Fifty elk cows were visible in the distance, and on the hills above the wolves were two herds of sheep totalling 58 animals, including 15 full-curl rams!"

Dekker believes that if wildlife populations are in trouble, hunting should be reduced. Fullerton is willing to consider restricting the number of sport hunting licences, but says that in areas less pristine than national parks wolf numbers have to be controlled too.

Some radicals in the hunting community periodically go so far as to call for wolf kills in Banff and Jasper national parks. They argue that wolves breed in the park and then spread onto provincial lands where they prey on game animals. What they fail to mention, of course, is that far more trophy elk, bighorn sheep and mule deer also wander out of the national parks, sustaining much of Alberta's finest hunting in the mountains along the park boundaries.

One fall I hunted a valley that I had never explored before. It was a bittersweet experience, because the valley bore many marks of the heavy hand of industrial man. Loggers had clearcut side-slopes, off-road vehicle tracks had eroded meadows and trails, and old camps were littered with garbage. I spent a lot of time just trying to find places where I could sustain the illusion of being in a wild landscape.

I took my little daughter out to explore an old logging road there one evening. We could hear a moose calf complaining about something in the old spruce timber as we wandered along the trail and studied the tracks of whitetails, moose and wolves in the wet spots.

The mountain peaks were pink with alpenglow when we arrived at a washed-out bridge over a small river. Evening had settled like a benediction over the valley. Bats flickered overhead. My daughter chattered happily at my side as I scanned the edges of the upstream beaver meadows.

Unexpectedly, just across the river, a long drawn-out howl reverberated from the dark timber. Katie's eyes widened. "A wolf," she whispered.

I nodded. Farther in, another wolf and then another took up the refrain. The valley roared with the resonance of their chorus.

Then it was over. The valley was utterly still. Animals everywhere, no doubt, were listening as we were, nerves tingling. Clearcuts were forgotten; eroded gullies and garbage piles suddenly irrelevant. In those few short moments a wounded valley had its wildness restored. Later that fall, the mule deer and elk I shot there seemed wilder and more precious for having survived in a place they shared with wolves; in fact, that valley will never look the same to me again.

Still, as my excited daughter and I traced our way back to the car through the darkening valley, I couldn't help but feel a little melancholy about the prospects for those wolves. Because although there were doubtless other hunters in the valley that evening who heard the howling of wolves, I suspect I may have been one of the very few who took pleasure in it.

Where Wolves Go to Die

 My daughter Katie, like most 11-year-olds, liked wolves. That's why she asked me to take her looking for wolf tracks one mild spring day.

"They're all dead," I said. Humans had recently reduced southwestern Alberta's tiny population of 50 or 60 wolves to fewer than 10. There was little point in looking for a wolf anywhere south of Banff.

Katie insisted, however, so we bundled up for the cold and set off into the winter woods on snowshoes. We soon cut the tracks of four coyotes. Following them, we found where they had hunted mice, frolicked in the snow and stopped to watch their back trail. As we returned along the half-frozen river one yapped at us from the forest.

I yelped back. A moment later two or three coyotes responded with a maniacal caterwauling.

As the echoes faded, I thought I heard a deeper voice in the distance. Katie stood stock-still, listening. She turned to me with a question on her face.

I howled. This time the wild and mournful answer that came resonating through the winter afternoon was unmistakable.

"I told you we'd find a wolf," Katie whispered.

Another wolf howled, closer, somewhere in the tangle of cottonwoods and willows nearby. The two conversed: long-drawn moans interspersed with deep barks. We were just about to move upstream and try to spot them when a third, deeper-voiced wolf howled right across the river.

We listened to the hair-lifting chorus for several minutes. Then, as the sun set behind Mount Crandell, we hurried back to the van. I drove to a roadside pull-off where we could glass the area. Small bunches of white-tailed deer and two groups of bull elk were feeding in the scattered meadows. Katie peered through our window-mounted spotting scope.

"The elk are running," she announced.

A grey wolf appeared at the edge of the aspens, trotting leisurely toward a cluster of elk. The elk ran a few metres then stopped as the wolf turned away. Now we could see a second grey wolf. Both rushed a group of deer. The deer darted away, then stopped and watched. Again the wolves abandoned the pursuit.

We watched, enthralled, as the two greys and a large black wolf tested several bunches of deer and elk in the fading evening light. When we got home later, Katie burst into the house to tell her mom and brothers the news: "Dad said we wouldn't find any wolves, but he was wrong!"

I knew, perhaps better than Katie, how privileged we had been to see these wolves in Waterton Lakes National Park. Four years earlier, wolves had denned in the park for the first time in half a century. They raised at least three pups in the summer of 1993. Next year, they raised seven.

By the following year, however, the Belly River wolf pack was gone, along with most of the other wolves in southern Alberta.

Salix, as Montana wolf biologist Diane Boyd had named the dominant female two years before she dispersed into Canada from her original home in Montana's Flathead River valley, was the only member of the Belly Pack to wear a radio collar. Wolf researchers found her bloodied radio collar hidden in bushes near a logging road east of the national park. A hunter had shot her.

Doubtless the same fate befell most of the pack, since their travels took them far afield into the heavily roaded public forestlands and ranching country of southwestern Alberta. All told, more than 40 wolves died at the hands of humans in 1994 and the following winter. By spring of 1995, wolf tracks no longer laced the spectacular aspen parkland country that spills east from the Rocky Mountains.

Exterminated from the region by a 1950s poisoning campaign, wolves from northern B.C. and Alberta finally dispersed south along the Rocky Mountains in the early 1980s. In 1986 many Americans were thrilled to learn that wolves had denned and raised pups in northern Montana for the first time in decades. Unlike wolves in Alberta, those colonizing wolves were protected under the U.S. Endangered Species Act. Only wolves that kill livestock can be shot or trapped in Montana, and then only by qualified Animal Damage Control officers. Since most Montana wolves are content with wild meat, the population has thrived.

Biologists estimate that northern Montana now has seven or eight packs totalling close to 80 wolves. In a sort of ecological free trade, Montana wolves began dispersing north in the 1990s, establishing new packs in the foothills of southern Alberta. Salix was one such disperser. So were two other young females originally radio-collared by Diane Boyd in Montana's Flathead Valley. Both drifted north in 1994 and became the founding females of the Beauvais and Carbondale packs, southwest of Pincher Creek in the Alberta foothills. Like Salix, both died at the hands of human hunters.

Out of the deathly silence that had settled on the Alberta foothills by early 1995, new wolf tracks finally reappeared early in 1996. Three new wolves had found their way into the game-rich Belly River country east of Waterton. They were the wolves Katie and I encountered.

Perhaps those wolves included survivors of the Belly Pack. Their tracks showed that they travelled the same hunting routes. Like the Belly Pack, their travels took them, occasionally, through a large field used by a local rancher as his calving pasture. A few weeks after Katie and I watched them interact with elk and deer, the wolves made the mistake of travelling through the calving pasture in daylight. By the time the last gunshot went rolling off into the windy distance, the big black male and his grey mate—pregnant with six pups—lay dead.

The killing of a pregnant female and her mate was legal under Alberta's wildlife regulations. The wolves were not harassing livestock; their bellies contained only the remains of wild prey. The wolves were simply shot on suspicion—business as usual in Alberta where, reasonable-sounding policy rhetoric notwithstanding, official regulations treat wolves as little better than vermin.

The killings, however, frustrated Dave Mihalic, superintendent of Montana's Glacier National Park. In an interview published in the local Waterton-Glacier Views, Mr. Mihalic said, "People say, well, you know, they only killed two wolves outside Waterton. No: they killed eight wolves—two adults and six pups—the pups just weren't born yet. If those two wolves were the ones we think they were—they were in Many Glacier and St. Mary and East Glacier all last summer and fall— that means they wiped out Glacier's east-side wolf pack."

Alberta's wolf management plan, formally released in 1993, should give Mr. Mihalic some comfort. In support of the wildly popular wolf recovery plan for the northern U.S. Rockies, Alberta's official wolf policy commits the government to maintaining a population of 50 wolves south of Calgary. To reduce the risk that those wolves might come into conflict with ranchers in the productive foothills region, the policy promises cash compensation for anyone who loses livestock to wolves. It also provides for speedy removal of wolves that develop a taste for Alberta beef.

Alberta's plan should comfort Mr. Mihalic, but it probably doesn't. Words are cheap. Alberta's policy may sound enlightened but its actual regulations are not.

No sooner was the ink dry on the new wolf policy than Alberta's legislators, caught up in a frenzy of cost-cutting, struck the already-existing livestock compensation program from the books. As of March 1993, Alberta ranchers were on their own to cope with the financial costs— sometimes substantial—when predators killed cows or sheep. Then, when wolves began to kill cattle in the Chain Lakes area southwest of Calgary, predator control officers were unable to find and eliminate the wolves responsible. One reason: no provincial money to pay for radio-collaring wolves so officers could track their movements. The cattle losses continued unabated for almost a year.

Recognizing that the growing cost of cattle losses could create a backlash against all wolves, not just the ones doing the killing, the Waterton Natural History Association and the Canadian Parks and Wilderness Society stepped into the vacuum created when the provincial government abandoned its compensation program. They canvassed their members and the public to raise funds for reimbursing ranchers the full value of their lost livestock. The new program was controversial, however: some ranchers refused to take money from environmental groups, fearing there might be strings attached. Others felt that compensation should come from government and be available to all Alberta ranchers, not just those in the southwest. Others stubbornly insisted that there simply should be no wolves. Finally, in 1996, the provincial government reinstated its old province-wide compensation program.

The hollowness of the words in Alberta's wolf management policy, however, became most starkly clear in 1994 and 1995. By 1994, mostly because of wolves dispersing north out of Montana, southern Alberta finally met its wolf population target. Biologists estimated a total population of 50 or 60 wolves, including the Belly, Beauvais and Carbondale packs.

But things soon went awry. Monitoring reports about the radio-collared wolves created new public awareness that wolves were back in southwestern Alberta. As rural residents began spotting wolves where they had not seen any before, the uneasy feeling grew that wolf numbers were increasing too fast. Media coverage of the cattle losses near the Whaleback added fuel to those concerns. A well-known local hunter, Horst Fauser, fanned the flames in a widely distributed update on wildlife conditions in southern Alberta: "There is an abundance of wolves and they enjoy cattle north of Highway 3—maybe no ungulates left? The Belly River pack will soon run out of deer as well."

As if the local media coverage were not enough, national and international media were full of stories about a controversial plan to transplant Alberta and B.C. wolves to Yellowstone National Park in the U.S.

When hunting season opened in 1994, many hunters were gunning for wolves, worried about competition from a predator that has no closed season. Growing numbers of ranchers, too, began to carry rifles in their trucks. As the snow grew deep, trappers headed back into the hills with visions of long-haired wolf pelts to be had.

By spring 1995, almost all the wolves in the area were dead. Trappers had killed 15. A truck killed one on a highway west of Pincher Creek. Wildlife officers trying to stem the losses of cattle poisoned four and shot one. Ranchers shot several. Hunters shot most of the rest during the fall hunting season.

The wolf packs that had the best records for avoiding conflict with ranchers, ironically, suffered worst. The open country and abundant roads between Pincher Creek and Waterton Lakes National Park made it impossible for the Belly, Beauvais and Carbondale packs to stay out of sight long. That, coupled with Alberta's lax hunting regulations, sealed their fates.

Not that those fates bothered some ranchers. "Our grandparents went to a lot of trouble to get rid of wolves," one said. "Why would we want to let them come back now?"

The prevailing sentiment that wolves don't belong in ranching country has deep roots. When settlers first brought cattle to western ranges a century ago bison were newly extinct, elk had virtually disappeared and deer were rare. Early ranchers left their cattle and horses free to range over vast areas, and desperate wolves soon learned to kill them.

Today, however, elk, deer and other wild prey are so common that Alberta and other provinces are unable to sell all the available hunting licences. In parts of southwestern Alberta, for example, hunters who apply for a doe mule deer licence receive two tags instead of one: the result of too many deer and too few predators. Horst Fauser's rhetorical lament over the fate of southern Alberta's ungulate herds—some of which are at near-record levels—rings hollow as desperate herds of hundreds of mule deer and elk descend on ranchers' hay yards each winter.

Ranchers manage their stock differently now, too. Most cows give birth to their calves in protected fields rather than out on the open range. Ranchers closely tend their herds in winter. Some clean up the carcasses of cows and sheep that die of natural causes, rather than leaving them out where wolves scavenging the remains might be drawn into too-close contact with live animals.

Research has also yielded new understanding of wolves over the past century. Wolves, it turns out, are not random killers. Like dogs, wolves learn through experience to do things most likely to yield a reward. Consequently, most wolf packs develop hunting patterns that select for specific kinds of prey. For example John Gunson, retired Alberta provincial carnivore specialist, studied two wolf packs in the 1970s. He found that one pack killed mostly elk while the other killed mostly moose, even though both ranged through the same area. They weren't random killers; each pack had a specialty.

Why did neither the Belly River or Beauvais wolf packs choose to kill the numerous cows and calves they encountered during the course of their daily hunts? Why did the short-lived wolf pack that reappeared in the Belly Pack's former range in 1996 also choose to pass up beef? Probably the wolves simply did not recognize cows as desirable prey. They were looking for what they had hunted successfully before: deer and elk.

Unlike the rancher who shot the wolves near Waterton in the spring of 1997, Bonnie Gardner knows what it's like to lose valuable livestock to wild predators. Even so, she and her husband could never kill a wolf just because it's there.

"We have to make room for nature," she says. "It's too easy to try and solve your troubles by just killing things. But if you take that far enough, you just end up sterilizing the landscape. No one can live in a sterile landscape."

Her husband Francis agrees. "Wolves are an important part of the whole system. We need them out there."

The Gardners, however, are no blind idealists. They know that the wrong wolf pack can run a productive ranch into the red. "I've lost all kinds of stock to wolves over the years," says Francis.

Windburned and thoughtful, Francis Gardner is like many second- and third-generation Alberta ranchers. He takes pride in the health of his land and the abundant wildlife it supports. Normally, he is philosophical about the fact that his good management means wolves inevitably will turn up sooner or later. When wolves kill his livestock however, Mr. Gardner's live-and-let-live philosophy gives way to pragmatism. He can't afford to lose those cows.

"I only recall two cases where I had to take action about wolves. The worst one was when a pack killed eight head over two weeks in 1994. I could hear the commotion in the night—cows bawling and coyotes in the distance making all kinds of weird noises. That time I called Fish and Wildlife and they put in a poison bait station and killed three wolves. The other time was in early 1995. We lost two yearling heifers a week apart. There was only one wolf that time and they never got it."

The Gardners received World Wildlife Fund Canada's prestigious Alberta Prairie Conservation Award in 1995, only a few months after their last livestock loss to wolves. The award recognized the couple's long commitment to preserving prairie grassland—among the most endangered ecosystems in Canada—and protecting native biodiversity on a working cattle ranch. The Gardners market organically raised beef. They helped pioneer the use of fire to restore natural processes to foothills grasslands. Recently, they changed their grazing patterns to restore ecological health to their streams and riparian areas. Their ranch is a demonstration site to help educate others about progressive range management practices.

Even so, when they need to—but only when they need to—they ask Alberta Environment officers to kill wolves on their ranch.

Francis Gardner feels that managing wolves in cattle country should be a fairly straightforward business. "Give the officers authority to control the wolves that do the killing. Protect the ones that don't. If you can compensate for the killings, then a lot of ranchers won't be so touchy. And it would help if you could let ranchers know how wolves fit into the scheme of things, educate them about wolves, so they can make their own decisions. The big mistake is the people and groups who try to impose solutions on ranchers."

It's a simple prescription. Wolf biologists agree it would work. However, Alberta's antiquated regulations guarantee continued failure. Virtually anyone can kill as many wolves as they want, regardless of whether those wolves hunt cattle or live on wild game. Alberta regulations currently state that:

• any landowner may shoot a wolf at any time on or within eight kilometres of his or her land

• any Albertan, without a licence, may shoot a wolf on land to which they have right of access for approximately nine months of each year (September through May)

• trappers may kill as many wolves as they wish

After the 1994/1995 bloodbath, when Alberta's existing wildlife regulations led to the death of almost 90 percent of the wolves south of Calgary, provincial biologists drafted new regulations to reduce random losses of wolves to hunters. They proposed:

- a wolf hunting licence that would entitle holders to kill only one wolf per year
- a reduced wolf open season, from nine to six months, to protect wolves during the denning season
- mandatory reporting by hunters, trappers or landowners of all wolves killed
- an annual quota for human-caused wolf mortality, with notification to licensed hunters when the quota is reached and hunting season for that year closed
- that trappers voluntarily comply with closed seasons
- no change to landowner right to kill wolves on or near his or her property

The proposed wolf regulation changes received widespread public support, as might be expected in the wake of so many well-publicized wolf deaths. Unfortunately, Alberta's then-Minister of Environmental Protection Ty Lund rejected the proposed changes. The regulations remain unchanged.

Wolves will continue to disperse into southwestern Alberta's prime foothills habitat. Some may come from Montana's expanding population. Others may come from B.C. or farther north in Alberta. They will find abundant prey, lightly populated landscapes and a community divided over how to live with wolves. They will know nothing about Alberta's Wolf Management Plan, nor will they understand that every human they meet can legally kill them.

Soon after they arrive, they will die.

Choices and Values

Nature Proofing for
Allergic Hunters

One summer afternoon I experienced a revelation. It occurred as I sat in my backyard, musing about the impending hunting season. We lived then at the very edge of a bedroom community south of Calgary. Across the back fence was a full half section of land under development for a housing subdivision. The developer had stripped the vegetation, rearranged the contours and was busy pouring concrete, sod and houses over top of a network of buried pipes, power conduits and drains.

Watching the earthmovers obliterate all traces of the original landscape, it came to me: North Americans are allergic to nature. We have evolved to a higher plane.

Like all great revelations, the moment I realized this simple truth, many things that had once puzzled me became clear. And like others who have experienced great revelations before me, I recognized my responsibility to share this newfound wisdom with others.

Fortunately, the great majority of people need not worry much about their allergy if they don't venture out looking for nature. Today it is perfectly possible to avoid all contact with nature. We've successfully eliminated it from large parts of the landscape. Bioengineering and other new technologies are increasingly limiting nature's role even in producing the things we eat. Most people can walk on asphalt, breathe air-conditioned air, drink chlorinated water, eat genetically modified and irradiated foods, and watch life through a television screen-avoiding any risk of an allergic reaction.

Among the rest of us—who risk the allergic reaction and actually seek out nature—are hunters. We who pursue are particularly vulnerable to this allergy since the animals we hunt, poorly evolved creatures that they are, live in places simply inundated with nature.

We can practise safe sex, street-proof our kids, never open e-mail attachments, put automatic door locks and garage openers in our cars-we can protect ourselves from many of the perils of life in the 21st century. But how can we nature-proof our hunting?

Fortunately, modern technology offers many choices to allergic hunters who, lacking the money to buy their way into a sporting-clays club or other pre-engineered hunting environment, are forced against all their better inclinations to venture into nature.

To begin with, the allergic hunter has various forms of motor vehicle at his disposal. Many of those vehicles come with the option of tinted window glass that can serve to disguise the natural colours of the world outside. Loud country-and-western or rock music works well to drown out birdcalls or the annoying sounds of wind and water. Four-wheel drive enables the hunter to venture far into nature without actually having to make physical contact with it. When the truck will go no farther, a wide range of motorized tricycles, quads and trail bikes is available to continue to protect the allergic hunter from actual contact with the actual earth.

This is good, because in nature the ground is unpleasantly bumpy, sometimes slick and often cluttered. Clearly, given how untidy and disorganized it all is, wild nature was a hurried first draft. Of course, given that there were only six days to get it all done, it isn't fair to expect much more; nonetheless, it's fortunate that we humans came along in the fullness of evolutionary time to tidy things up. Unfortunately for allergy sufferers, however, the job isn't quite finished. That's why it's so helpful to have a wide variety of motor vehicles to protect one from having to deal with the inconvenience of possible stumbles or muscle fatigue. There is also the matter of fresh air; in a motor vehicle this unpleasant substance can be avoided entirely whereas on foot one is stuck with letting that stuff right into your lungs.

Unfortunately, there are sometimes fences or even trees standing in the way when modern hunters venture forth across the landscape on their motorized steeds. This is where wire cutters, chain saws and other forms of technology prove their worth. Winches and chains are among other handy little gadgets that help overcome the difficulties imposed by Mother Nature's irksome failure to level the landscape.

Inevitably the hunter with a nature allergy faces the final conundrum: an animal or bird that must be shot. Genetic engineering hasn't arrived in the wilds yet (although game ranchers may soon remedy this, especially if they continue to build the breakable fences that are now industry standard), so there can be no avoiding the unpleasant fact that nature and wildlife remain synonymous even today, in spite of all the advances of modern civilization.

One way to minimize the exposure is to use a firearm that has been sighted in at 350 metres or more. Ideally, the allergic hunter should barely be able to distinguish the animal at which he is shooting. This also improves the chances of simply wounding the animal and thus avoiding the need ever to touch it.

If an allergic hunter drops an animal, the question of gutting it arises. This is a real challenge; even rubber gloves and a surgeon's face mask do little to reduce the hunter's exposure to real nature once he's got to reach inside that thing. Fortunately, gutting one's animal can be avoided entirely if you're careful not to shoot the animal too far from town. Many meat processing outfits will take a freshly killed big game animal straight from the back of a pickup truck, skin it, hang it, process, wrap and freeze it. Play your cards right and you might not even have to touch the thing.

An allergic hunter, thanks to modern technology, motorized vehicles, synthetic clothing and so forth, can manage to avoid any significant contact with nature. Modern humans with nature allergies can still be hunters if they have a detailed understanding of how to fix a 4X4, the ballistics of a .308, the price of beer, the workings of a winch and the merits of camo over blaze orange, while knowing next to nothing about wild animals or their habitat.

There are, however, still a few hunters who have managed to avoid this widespread allergy. They actually choose to hunt on foot-on unimproved terrain, no less. They visit nature—willingly, no less—before the season on scouting trips. They pass up difficult shots even though that means extending the period when they have to be exposed to green vegetation, wind and all that other earthy stuff. These hunters stalk to within close range of their prey, and actually gut, skin and haul it out on foot, and then butcher it too! By choice!

These primitive throwbacks study the lay of the land, get to know the names of common plants, are curious about the birds and other wildlife they see, and all too frequently join conservation organizations to help protect nature. This sort of hunter clearly does not belong in the civilized world of the 21st century and should be avoided by allergic hunters at all costs. It seems reasonable to assume, after all, that to be allergic to nature means being allergic to anyone who actually likes it.

The problem is, if you actually go hunting you can never tell when you might meet a non-allergic hunter. You can't always tell by looking at them. Given the risks, the best solution for hunters who are allergic to nature may be simply to stay home and watch a video of somebody else hunting. There are some very affordable little hunting computer games too. This is the kind of solution I'd recommend.

The rest of us don't want you out there anyway. At least, not until that allergy clears up.

Licence to Abuse

W ild pigs!" my daughter exclaimed. "Look at all the babies!"A neighbour had fenced off a few acres of coulee and stocked it with wild boars. As I braked on the curve, the kids craned their necks to look at the exotic animals. Large brown adults rooted beneath saskatoon bushes and buckbrush. Striped piglets scurried about in pursuit of their mothers.

From time to time over the following months we drove by the wild hog farm. Each time the herd had grown by another litter or two, and each time the coulee looked a lot worse for wear. By late summer the land looked like it had been strip-mined. Big barren patches were sprouting thistles. Saskatoons were wilting, roots exposed to the sun. The coulee bottom was mud. The clear stream of water that flowed into the enclosure was algal scum by the time it oozed out. What had been productive, healthy land had been abused into devastation.

The pigs are gone now because the municipal government finally stepped in. They didn't take the owner to task for his abuse of the land, however; they closed him down because the neighbours complained about water quality. Communities are seldom reluctant to create laws that protect human health and property values. Rarely, however, do they intervene to protect land from abusive owners.

Ownership is a strange concept. We use the same possessive pronoun to speak of our land, our homes, our families and our friends. All are ours, but we mean something different by "our" when we apply it to people than when we apply it to land. Land—although it is no less alive, responsive, generous and vulnerable than the people in our lives—is property. Our ownership of land, consequently, is too often the kind of cold and selfish relationship that would never be tolerated between people.

Abuse results from a perverted sense of the rights and responsibilities ownership entails. If I were to take the same approach to my family as too many take to their land, the community would not hesitate to call me to accounts. They may be mine, but I have no right to do them harm. I own my family not because I bought them, but because I love them and they, in turn, love me. The bond of love allows me to call them "mine" and them to call me "theirs." I earn that possessive pronoun by nurturing my relationship with them and placing their needs at least on a par with, if not above, my own. Their well-being always matters more to me than what I can get out of them.

If I were to buy or sell family members, my community would be revolted. We have laws against that. If I were to abuse them, fail to care for them, degrade them into less than what they should be, I would lose them. I would no longer have the moral right—or, if the authorities should find out—the legal right, to call them "mine."

So why does one kind of ownership look and feel so different from the other? Why, when we speak of "our" families do we concentrate on our responsibility to give, while when we speak of "our" land we concentrate on what we perceive to be our right to take? Why is abuse of one relationship absolutely unacceptable to the same neighbours and community who consider abuse of the other relationship normal and acceptable? There was a time when the community kept its eyes averted from what went on behind a family's closed doors. Thankfully, we've gotten beyond that and few hesitate to speak up against child or spousal abuse. Yet we still feel it inappropriate to speak out against another form of betrayal—abuse of land by those who believe ownership is more about rights than responsibilities.

Any Sunday drive reveals a lot to those who study fenceline contrasts. Here a cow-degraded creek bottom betrays the smug irresponsibility of a landowner who feels his title deed frees him of any obligation to native plants and animals. Over there, a flower-strewn bunchgrass prairie speaks quietly of an owner who ministers to the land rather than exploiting it. Here, chemical abuse shows up in weed-free acres of grain stubble. Across the fence, drained sloughs pockmark a tired field like cigarette burn marks. Dirt bike tracks slash the face of a hillside, but just across the way lush willow thickets echo with the happy sound of birdsong where an owner has sacrificed to keep her land healthy. Each fenceline reveals the attitude of another landowner.

Community standards evolve. There was a time, as Aldo Leopold pointed out half a century ago in his famous "Land Ethic" essay, when it was perfectly acceptable to kill off all one's human slaves. Until well into the 20th century, a wife was considered property whose sole duty was to honour and obey the man who owned her. Those times are gone, and the world is a better place for it. We recognize, and speak out against, such abuses of people.

But little public shame attaches to those who abuse land. We don't shun or accuse those who exploit and destroy habitat, if they can prove that they own it in fee simple. Ownership of land, in the community's eyes, amounts to licence to do almost anything the owner wishes. As Leopold wrote: "There is as yet no social stigma in the possession of a gullied farm, a wrecked forest or a polluted stream, provided the dividends suffice to send the youngsters to college."

Conservation groups rail against habitat loss, farming groups against soil erosion, environmental groups against water pollution and heritage groups against the loss of the landscape's aesthetic qualities. But for the most part, all ascribe to the view that a land title entitles its holder to do as he or she wishes to the property described thereon. This is why the view from the roadside, too often, is not a happy one.

We would all have a lot less worry if we could learn to recognize land ownership not as a right but as the profound and awesome responsibility it is. Buying land is like a wedding—it's the easy part. The most difficult, but ultimately most rewarding, part of the relationship comes after. In this sense, then, it is not by signing papers and handing over money that we earn the right to own land. We earn that right in the same way that we earn the right to call spouses or children our own—through love, sacrifice and acceptance of an abiding obligation of service. Abusive relationships whether with other people, with other creatures or with the land itself, are always ugly and always wrong. Loving relationships—relationships founded on giving as opposed to taking—are things of beauty and rightness. Thus far, we have failed to apply this simple truth to the concept of land ownership. The marks of that failure are everywhere.

Weeds and Wheels

Weeds like Russian knapweed, leafy spurge, musk thistle and cheatgrass choke many western wildlife ranges—an insidious kind of damage invisible to people who don't recognize the difference between healthy vegetation and weeds. B.C. range ecologist Don Gayton says that cheatgrass—a fire-prone and mostly inedible foreign grass—now blankets more than 16 million western hectares. Knapweed, a coarse flowering plant loved by honeybees and nothing else, has taken over at least 800,000 more hectares. Around Missoula, Montana and many other western towns, virtually no healthy native rangeland survives. It's all weeds: a total biological wasteland.

Most exotic weeds originated in Europe or Asia. Their seeds arrived in North America mixed into shipments of grain or vegetable seeds, or in bedding for domestic livestock. Once here, they could outcompete native plants because they arrived without the insects, fungi and diseases that control their populations back home. Weeds thrive best where humans disturb native vegetation. Forest roads are like infected knife wounds: they create ribbons of knapweed and thistle that spread these weeds far into forests. Logging disturbs soil too, allowing weedy infections to spread even more. If ranchers allow their livestock to overgraze riparian areas, weeds exploit the wounded bottomlands. Spring floods then spread those downstream to invade more wildlife ranges.

Some weeds are problems for farmers but not for the rest of us. Ox-eye daisy, Russian thistle and goosefoot rarely invade native vegetation but can become serious problems in cultivated hay and other crops. The most serious problems are plants like leafy spurge and knapweed that invade healthy habitat and crowd out the natives, creating degraded near-monocultures that are virtually useless to wildlife.

Although agriculture originally brought most of today's noxious weeds to our western landscapes, their spread today is usually associated with the internal combustion engine. When I worked in Waterton Lakes

National Park, wardens watched for new weed infestations along the edges of roads where tourists from Montana, Utah, Colorado and B.C. frequently pulled onto the grass while they watched bears and other wildlife. Weeds trapped in the wheel wells or undercarriages of vehicles fall off and take root in these trampled spots. Dangerously invasive weeds like musk thistle, sulphur cinquefoil and Klamath weed regularly appear beside parking lots and along roadsides, brought in by motor vehicles from afar.

At least in the front country some people are regularly on the lookout for weeds. A far more insidious problem is the spread of knapweed and other exotics into remote backcountry as a result of off-road vehicles. When recreationists bring their dirt bikes, quads and other off-road vehicles into foothills and mountain forests, they often bring weed seeds too—especially when those vehicles are caked with mud. Conservationists often lobby for restrictions on off-road vehicle use because of the loss of solitude, silence and undisturbed wildlife that has accompanied the recent increase in all-terrain vehicle use. We should be no less concerned about the spread of erosion sites and weeds, because habitat loss to weeds is often irreversible. Protests from special interests notwithstanding, there is nothing harmless about off-roading.

Wildlife experts consider weed invasion one of the most insidious threats facing western wildlife populations. "Nobody's quite caught on to how bad it is," says former United States Forest Service chief Jack Ward Thomas. "Of all the perils that we face in wildland natural resource management, exotic weeds is one of the most underestimated."

Poisonous herbicides can be effective at controlling the spread of weeds if management agencies and private property owners react quickly. Once an aggressive weed like knapweed or cheatgrass is well-established, however, it becomes almost impossible to control with chemicals. Agriculture Canada and the U.S. Department of Agriculture continue to search for and test insects and pathogens that attack weeds. Several kinds of flea beetle, weevil and moth, imported from Europe, have proven effective at controlling plants like leafy spurge and St. John's wort. Still, biological control is risky: insects imported to control weeds can become problems in their own right if they change their habits in North America and begin to attack native plants instead. A weevil released in North Dakota to kill exotic thistles, for example, nearly wiped out several native species.

In the long run, weeds are here to stay. Tomorrow's wildlife habitat can never again be like yesterday's. Even so, good land management can reduce the damage. Many western ranchers have figured out how to manage cows and sheep so that the animals cause little damage to native vegetation. Weeds find it hard to invade healthy rangeland. Although Alberta and B.C. forest services remain married to the bulldozer, the U.S. Forest Service has cut back its road-building program drastically. Fewer new roads and more sensitive logging methods may reduce the spread of weeds into remote forested areas.

Restrictions on off-road vehicle use are rarely popular-nothing seems better able to arouse the wrath of some locals than when land use agencies propose stricter access management. But if we value the health of our wild landscapes, we need to recognize the most serious vector of noxious weed infestations today is the motor vehicle. Denial has never been very helpful to the cause of conservation. Those who insist on being granted the freedom to play with motorized toys on public lands should, at the very least, be willing to give up a few June and August evenings to get out there and clean up the consequences. We owe that much, at a minimum, to the living landscapes that have been so generous to us. Conservation, ultimately, is not about what we perceive to be our rights: it will always be about what we must accept as our responsibilities.

The End of the Hunt?

I am a hunter. This is neither apology nor boast. It is simply a fact. I'm glad of it, immensely grateful, in fact—but constantly humbled by the burden of responsibility it imposes on me.

Many of my most meaningful experiences happened while afield. Almost everything I like about myself goes back, one way or another, to hunting. On the other hand, my most shameful failures were during hunts too—so hunting has contributed to whatever moral maturity I might have attained. I could never have been so successful a biologist, so passionate an environmentalist or so thoughtful a writer had I never ventured into the wild as a predator.

Hunting, in short, permeates every aspect of my being.

I believe that done well, with skill, ethical restraint and humble respect for the animals we hunt and for the nature of the predator-prey relationship, hunting is an honourable part of our culture. I hope I'm never forced to stop. Increasingly, however, I fear that day will come.

What will end hunting will be cold science, hot rhetoric and the continued failure of too many hunters to accept that ethics and ecology must be always central to our understanding of the hunt-not fine-sounding rhetoric applied decoratively to the edges.

Hunters and hunting groups often proclaim that the threats to hunting come from animal rights and anti-hunting groups. Paranoia, perhaps, is more convenient than staring into the mirror and confronting the problem face to face. We hunters, too often, are our own worst enemies.

This point came home to me most forcibly in 1999 when I watched hunters react to the Ontario government's hasty political decision to stop licensing hunters to kill black bears in spring. Hunters and outfitters indignantly, and correctly, argued that shooting bears over bait barrels causes no harm to bear populations. In fact, they argued, the spring hunt is a good management tool because baiting allows the shooter to examine his prey and ensure that it's a mature male.

Cold science was on their side. There was no shortage of hot rhetoric. But they failed to advance the cause of hunting—just the opposite, in fact.

Perhaps, in part, that was because they sought to defend the ethically indefensible.

Much of the debate was over orphaned cubs. Animal rights activists say spring hunting orphans newborn bears. Outfitters and hunters' groups argue that the spring hunt actually selects for male bears. I was at a bear management workshop the week the decision came down, so I took advantage of the opportunity to consult with several of North America's leading bear biologists. They told me both sides are right.

Mother bears that visit bait barrels frequently hide their newborn cubs first. They do it because baited bears are almost always fully aware of the nearby hunter but simply can't resist the food bait. Bait-shooters kill many more male bears than female, but females die too. Even experts can't consistently tell a male from a female.

That orphans nursing cubs. How many? Nobody knows.

Cold science concerns itself with populations, not individuals. From that point of view, a few cubs matter little if the population continues to thrive. Human compassion would suggest, however, that even one orphaned cub is too many. No hunter would ever argue that leaving nursing bear cubs to starve to death is ethical or right. None would do it purposely—yet some vehemently defend spring bear baiting which, by design, does just that.

Hunting is predation. The universal compact between predator and prey requires that prey must have a fair opportunity to escape and the predator must exercise skill and craft. This is how predation makes both the deer and the wolf stronger, elk and cougar cannier, and mallard and peregrine swifter. Predation is nature's way of honing both predator and prey to their finest edge.

If hunting is predation—if at its heart it is an ecological interaction that helps perfect both predator and prey—then it becomes hard to honestly define spring bear baiting as hunting. Baiting doesn't select for woodsmanship, craft, stealth, alertness, fitness or courage in the hunter. Nor does it kill the most vulnerable, inattentive, naive or blundering bears. Bears emerging from their winter dens have a massive energy deficit to make up; they've just burned off a quarter of their body weight. No spring bear can turn down a free meal.

Killing a baited bear is a sordid, ugly act that has nothing in common with hunting. It degrades both predator and prey. It looks like hunting, but it is a pathetic and shameful facsimile.

In the United States, electors in many states have delivered this message to hunters, hunting groups and the cold science agencies that serve those hunters. Spring killing of bears over bait is illegal in California, Colorado, New Mexico and Minnesota, to name only a few of the states that now ban non-fair-chase hunting practices.

Indignant hunting groups blame the loss of bear baiting on slick ad campaigns by anti-hunting groups, and mass hysteria by an uninformed and biologically naive public. Some suspect a conspiracy to ban all hunting. Their spokesmen fume and rage in front of the media. They forget that we are, after all, a very small minority in a democratic society—and that our tolerance of unethical practices helped produce the ugly images those ad campaigns exploit.

Tom Beck is a devoted hunter who pursues deer, antelope and elk each fall with his bow. He's also one of the world's leading experts on black bear biology. For more than 20 years he has worked for the Colorado Division of Wildlife.

"I've been in the business long enough to know that there's an awful lot that's legal that isn't moral, and isn't ethical and isn't appropriate," he says. Beck's name evokes scorn and anger in some hunting circles because his understanding of bear biology and serious concern for hunting ethics has led him to speak publicly against spring bear hunting.

"You know," he says, "We keep getting mad because we don't like management by initiative or management by the legislature. But when you're unresponsive to what the general public wants that's what you're going to get. It's like education. What you hear over and over again from the hunters who are upset is: 'You guys in the division, you gotta go educate the poor stupid public as to what's right.' Well, there's no right or wrong. It's all value system—and we happen to have one that's out of step with a whole bunch of folks. These groups don't want to educate; they want to propagandize."

Another American hunter, Aldo Leopold, widely hailed as the father of modern wildlife management, would not have been surprised. In 1949 he wrote: "I have the impression that the...sportsman is puzzled; he doesn't understand what is happening to him...Wildlife administrators are too busy producing something to shoot at than to worry much about the cultural value of the shooting...."

Things have become no simpler in the half century since Leopold published his famous A Sand County Almanac with its eloquent plea for ecological wisdom and ethical restraint. Wild country has shrunken. Off-road vehicles have opened up the hinterland. New technologies enable hunters to find prey by their infrared signatures or amplified sound. Global positioning systems, pheronome scents, animal calls, laser sights and night vision optics put space-age science into the woods. Bait barrels dot black bear country and "hunting" clubs buy truckloads of rotting vegetables to attract white-tailed deer into rifle range.

Prairie Canada even has a private lottery that pays out big money for trophy heads. The "Ultimate Whitetail Challenge" turns living animals into poker chips, and hunters into gamblers. Like other perversions of our hunting tradition, it's legal. Legal, however, is not the same as right.

The problem is that the same anti-nature, exploitive world view that dominates so much of consumer culture has come to permeate hunting culture too. It's only natural that it would, after all. But there was a time when hunters organized to fight against the cheapening of our hunting heritage—to demand sportsmanship and fair chase in hunting. It was hunting groups, not animal rights groups, who fought successfully in the early 1900s to ban commercial trade in wildlife, outlaw baiting and end the spring hunting of waterfowl and other wildlife. What a difference a century makes.

Today, too many hunting groups seem ready to tolerate—or embrace—almost anything a government will legalize. Governments, in turn, have shown a pathetic willingness to legalize almost any practice that a commercial interest, bear hunt outfitters or game farm speculators, for example, will lobby them for. So we drift, ethical anchors dragging, into a future where hunters and hunting look less and less acceptable to society as a whole.

Is there a solution?

I believe there is. It is, however, almost the exact opposite of what the most vocal hunting groups have done to date over issues like the Ontario ban on killing spring black bears. It has four elements:

1. No more verbal attacks on animal rights groups. We share with those groups a common love for wild nature. We need to admit that the hunting community has failed to attend to some serious ethical issues. Hunters cheapen and degrade both our prey and ourselves when we use technology or tactics that overpower or bypass the natural defences of our prey. It's time to get out ahead of the animal rights groups and expunge practices—legal or otherwise—that are intrinsically unfair, shallowly competitive or potentially cruel.

2. Hunters need to set aside the elitist and offensive position that our woes are because of an ignorant urban, non-hunting public. Instead, we should listen to non-hunters carefully and with respect. Those animals we are privileged to hunt belong to everyone, if they belong to anyone. Community standards change. Hunting's continued existence depends on the tolerance of a much larger non-hunting majority. We'd better know what they consider honourable behaviour.

3. Hunters must exorcise the Ted Nugents of the hunting world who fill the media with hot rhetoric and angry images. Marshall McLuhan said, "The media is the message." Yelling into a camera, no matter how lucidly, is simply free advertising for the anti-hunting movement: "See, we told you all hunters are aggressive, hostile rednecks!" Hunters need humble, honest spokespeople who will demonstrate that we care deeply about animal welfare, ethics and integrity.

4. Most importantly, we need to rethink the nature of hunting and our role as hunters. As Tom Beck frequently points out, hunting—cold

science's ruling myths notwithstanding—is not the engine that drives wildlife management. It is merely one possible output. Bears regulate their own numbers without hunters. Pheasants don't need to be shot. Other predators could do as good or better a job on deer or elk numbers, if we were prepared to let them. Using wildlife management arguments to promote hunting simply doesn't stand up to critical scrutiny.

Yet, hunting is profoundly important—as part of our culture, and part of our ecology. At its best—but only at its best—it produces insightful ecologists, fiercely dedicated conservationists, deeply connected human beings.

At its best, hunting is ecologically grounded in the eternal compact between predator and prey: an ongoing partnership that brings out the best attributes of both hunter and hunted. At its best, hunting is built on the fundamental principle of fair chase, whereby the prey always has an advantage over the hunter. And at its best, it is always, unfailingly, grounded in ethical restraint, humble respect and human decency.

At its best, hunting may survive.

At its worst, however, it is both damned, and doomed.

Hunting With the Kids

Corey blinked groggily up at me in the near-darkness. I held a finger to my lips. "Don't wake your Mom," I whispered. "Hunting time." His eyes widened and, suddenly awake, he sat up and stretched. Katie didn't stir until I tickled the bottom of her foot.

By the time my son and daughter arrived blinking at the kitchen table, I had fresh coffee in the thermos and the back door open as I loaded the van in the dark. The chill air outside was full of the smell of frost and fallen leaves. Lisa, our golden retriever, whined and wagged her tail. She knew what that smell meant. She and I were going hunting with the kids again.

Like my own kids, I started hunting when I was about eight or nine. I was the second oldest of 10 children. Most of us, at one time or another, accompanied Dad into the irrigation farming country where he grew up. Saturdays during hunting season were sacred; whoever was going along with Dad that day would be up well before daybreak and home-socks full of burrs and dried thistles, eyes burning from sun and wind-well after dark.

Back then, most families included a hunter or two. There were no firearms acquisition certificates, no training requirements before a kid could buy his or her first licence and no real difficulties finding a place to hunt. I can't recall ever wondering if hunting was right or wrong; it was just part of how we lived.

Hunting trips soon became a passion for me; nothing else immersed me so thoroughly and intimately in wild nature. Only now, looking back from the perspective of middle age, do I know that those early hunting trips were moral training ground too.

Afield, I learned about responsibility and the consequences of bad decisions. Each Saturday was a dawn-to-dusk series of small lessons as I tagged along with Dad or, later, hunted alone along the irrigation canals and coulees. I wounded a coyote once, and have never forgotten the remorse and self-loathing that followed me home that day. Although I didn't realize it then, I had learned an indelible lesson about the power of humans arbitrarily to impose pain or death. The memory of that animal's suffering has stopped me many times since from pulling the trigger frivolously. My ethical education was strengthened by repeatedly witnessing the respect my Dad showed for other people's property, or his refusal to abandon the search for a wounded pheasant until we had scoured every inch of possible hiding cover several times over.

Dad is gone now, and so too are the days when most kids grew up with hunting. Fewer than seven percent of all Canadians now take up guns or bows each fall in pursuit of game. Most of us live in cities and large towns, disconnected from the wild. Perhaps our isolation helps explain why concern for the environment is higher than ever before-certainly higher than when I was a kid. Part of that concern for the environment is expressed by a growing movement to ban hunting. Hunting, in many people's minds, is exploiting nature: killing wild animals for fun. When hunters try to explain the complex reasons why we really hunt, our efforts, too often, sound like little more than weak rationalization.

Looking at the bright faces of my two oldest children as they scrambled into the backseat, I felt grateful to know that they had chosen to come with me into the field this morning. They might never end up carrying a gun afield in years to come, but at least now, in their formative years, they would be out in the real and living world with a father who hunts.

We drove east through the darkness. Katie sat forward, eagerly watching for animals in the headlights while Corey huddled into the warmth of his jacket, still waking up.

"Stop, Dad! Look!" Katie cried. Something small zigzagged crazily across the pavement then stopped, frozen in the headlight glare at the edge of the shoulder. It was a deer mouse. I waited while the kids leaped out of the car and crouched over it. Katie reached out to touch the dazzled creature, but it scurried away into the grass.

Later we saw owls, a jackrabbit, a few deer. The eastern horizon paled and a rich orange glow began to pool along the skyline. At length we slowed then turned off the pavement onto the crunch of gravel. I pulled over to the edge of the road, uncased my gun and shook some shot shells into my pocket. The wind was sharp on my face as I stood beside the van, bemused; this was what my own dad used to do. In some ways I've never really stopped feeling like one of the bright-eyed crew now waiting for me to get back inside, but the years have flown; now I am become the father I remember.

We had no sooner pulled out onto the grid road than a flock of Hungarian partridges erupted from the edge of the road and sailed into a nearby stubble field.

"I saw where they landed, Dad!"

A decade or so ago I would have skidded to a stop and piled out after those birds. The field wasn't posted and there were no nearby houses. But things change as one's values mature.

"I don't know whose field this is," I replied. "There'll be more."

"But I can see them, Dad. They're right there! They're looking at us."

"Well, see if you can spot some more after this next corner. We have permission to hunt there."

Katie sulked, but only until we saw an owl on a fencepost. It waited until we slowed to watch it then spread its wings and dropped to fly along the fenceline a few hundred metres, then veered up and settled on a power pole. Its head pivoted to watch us go by. The kids stared back.

Owls were scarce in pheasant country when I was the kid trying to persuade my father to ignore "No Trespassing" signs. Those we did see were often dead, hanging with their wings tangled around the barbed wire of roadside fences. In those days, many hunters considered hawks and owls competition and had no compunction about filling them with duck shot. Coyotes were little better off-all Dad had to do was put his foot on the brake for a watching coyote to take off across the prairie like all the demons in hell were on its tail. Even then, Dad never killed predators; now, few other hunters do either.

The first time I ever saw my dad excited was one morning when we saw three mule deer. He pulled over to the side of the road and we watched as the strange creatures pogo-sticked over a rise and out of sight. Dad had grown up in the countryside where he took us hunting, and had never seen a deer there before. I remember thinking it strange to see my own father jabbering like a kid; that wasn't any part of how I thought I knew him.

Years later, I realized that I would have never have known my father in the same way if we hadn't hunted together. Maybe I never would have really known him at all.

The sun was well up by the time we parked in front of the "Use Respect" sign and stepped out into the wind. Lisa bounded about excitedly, tail wagging. The creek valley stretched away to the south, tangles of rose and buckbrush alternating with dense thickets of willow. Overhead, geese were gabbling. I pointed out the long wavering lines to the kids but they had already spotted them.

"Let's go," I said, parting the barbed wire. The dog was already in the bushes, still bouncing her first burst of energy out of her system. As I stepped over the top strand of the fence there was an explosion of noise and the startled cackle of a flushing cock pheasant. I sent a hopeless charge of shot after the bird then saw Lisa bounding along the creek hot on another scent. I started to run, but it was too late; another cock and three hens lifted from the far corner and sailed up the valley and out of sight with Lisa in hot pursuit.

There was a time when I would have been furious. Instead, I shook my head and muttered, "Idiot dog." Corey laughed.

By the time Lisa returned, panting hard and covered with burrs, we were well away from the road. Tree sparrows lisped in the undergrowth. Katie had stopped to study some raccoon tracks in the mud. Corey was practising on leaves with his BB gun, dawdling along on a parallel course to his sister and me. I didn't bother scolding the dog; she wouldn't have understood. Instead I waved her into a long oxbow crowded with willow and hawthorn.

Shortly later I heard a startled cackle, then nothing, then the explosion of a rising pheasant. Gaudy and sleek, a big cock pheasant towered out above the willows and arced away toward the far side of the creek.

My shotgun boomed, and the bird crumpled into the brush.

"Fetch!"

"He got it! You got it, Dad!"

That was my daughter, who only last year had told me hunters were cruel. She joined me to watch Lisa deliver the bird to my hand, and asked if she could carry it. I knew I'd have it back soon. I well remember how quickly a pheasant grows heavy in an 11-year-old's hand and how the hardened spurs on its legs dig into soft flesh.

There was a time when I couldn't imagine taking kids hunting with me. I was too full of hunting urge. I wanted to cover the miles, to hunt from dawn to dusk and come home with a limit of whatever I was after. My kids were babies then. Hunting was something I did away from the responsibilities of home.

But it didn't take too many seasons before I began to realize that those hunting trips were incomplete. However rich the day might have been, there was a hollow in its heart. My own dad had only hunted alone when there were no kids available; with 10 of us, that was seldom indeed. My children had become older during the seasons when I went off on my own—not able to keep up with me but old enough to like exploring nature and to keep themselves entertained during long drives.

I started taking them along on sharp-tailed grouse hunts in the open bunchgrass country of the foothills. Parking them in a clump of bushes with strict orders not to stray, I hunted a wide circle across country, keeping an eye on them from afar. Alone together in what must have felt like wilderness, they discovered chickadees, made hiding places for their stuffed animals and invented elaborate stories with which they then regaled me during the drive to our next hunting spot.

As the kids became older, they sometimes tagged along for part of each day before finding some interesting place to explore until the dog and I came wandering back. Sometimes they flushed their own grouse or pheasants by mistake. Once, when their younger brother Brian was along on his first trip, the three kids cornered a cottontail rabbit in an old outhouse and tried to pet it. Another time they surrounded two raccoons. Fortunately, they had enough sense not to try petting them.

Coming home, each day's adventures spill out breathlessly on the kitchen table along with whatever birds their father has been lucky enough to hit that day. Their mom listens with patient amusement, just as my mother listened to other children a few decades ago.

Years from now, I suspect, each of my children will know themselves, in part, by the memories they gathered, the lessons they learned and the landscapes to which they bonded while hunting with their dad. That, after all, is how he has come to know himself.

I think that if I didn't have my own kids, I'd have to borrow some.

Shortly after that trip, our family sat down to a Sunday dinner of fried pheasant and garden potatoes. Hunting season was over for another year. Lisa lay in her corner of the kitchen, twitching in her sleep. I could see some burdock burrs I had missed after our last hunting trip tangled behind one ear. The kids were talking about Corey's Canyon, as they have come to call one of our secret pheasant coulees.

"So," I began, "Should I be thinking about getting you shotguns for next year? Corey and Katie will both be old enough to hunt."

Katie stared at me, startled by the immensity of the thought. Then she said, "No way! I would never shoot things."

Corey shook his head, too, but his eyes were pensive.

I asked, "So you don't want to go hunting after all?"

"Of course we want to go hunting," Katie corrected me. "It's fun."

That's good enough for me. For now. Taking kids afield doesn't require making hunters out of them. What's more important is to make people out of them. I can't think of a better way than to take them hunting—helping them form their own lasting bonds with wild nature, develop a sense of freedom and independence, and learn the ethics of restraint and responsibility. Even if none of my kids ever chooses to shoot a gun, I suspect that they already are hunters in the most important ways.

Even so, I'm watching out for a good used 20-gauge. If history is any guide, I have a feeling there could be an argument over who gets to use it first, come next fall.

The Nature of the Place

Tomorrow's Trout

Meadow Creek is a tiny creek that winds through quiet meadows at the foot of the Rocky Mountains. One day Dad saw a submarine there.

Dad wasn't one of those fishermen whose fish continue to grow each time the story's told, so each time he retold his story I would stare awestruck at that tiny stream, so narrow that you could jump across it.

The submarine, apparently, had revealed itself to him as he peered into a deep hole where a bank beaver den had long ago caved in, leaving a narrow nick in the deeply undercut bank. First its head appeared, grey and malevolent looking. The head vanished on the upstream side of the nick, and white-edged fins followed it. Then its back went past forever, followed by two more white-edged fins and finally by a broad tail that waved a lazy goodbye as it passed from sight beneath the undercut bank.

He always described it as a submarine. "But how big was it really?" I asked in frustration. I wanted numbers.

He spread his arms then shrugged. "I don't know," he said. "It looked as big as a submarine. Close to three feet, I guess."

Dad's hands shook as he inched along the bank and eased his lure beneath the bank where the monster had vanished. It was to no avail; the great fish may have found its way into our family legends but it never found its way into Dad's creel.

The story was true, but no matter how far I hiked along that creek or how carefully I sneaked up on its most promising pools, the best I could ever find were 25-centimetre cutthroats and fat little brookies. The submarine was gone.

Johnson Creek, a nearby meadow stream we often fished for its small cutthroats, produced my first clue as to the identity of Dad's submarine, on one of those flawless summer mornings when the meadows are alive with birdsong and trout are rising eagerly in each sunlit pool. One large pool seemed strangely fishless. Near its head, I managed to hook a 15-centimetre fish but before I could lift it from the water, the little guy darted into a tangle of logs and stopped dead.

Resigned to the loss of a hook, I pulled hard to break the leader. Whatever I was snagged on gave a little, then reluctantly slid out from beneath the jam.

As it emerged into sunlight my heart nearly stopped; the snag was a huge trout, hanging onto the now-dead cutthroat with grim determination.

I backed up the bank and the great fish slid, barely resisting, onto the grass. Pouncing, I clubbed him with a rock. Only once I was sure that he wasn't going to escape did I realize that the 45-centimetre trout hadn't even been hooked; he'd just been stubbornly refusing to let go of his meal.

I was both exhilarated and disappointed. We had never seen so huge a fish in that little creek, but it was only a bull trout.

Bull trout were always a kind of paradox to those of us who grew up fishing the creeks and rivers of western Alberta. The really big monsters that our parents and grandparents told us about were always bull trout, so in some ways the bull trout was a symbol of the wildest and finest of places, and of the hidden possibilities of those headwaters streams. But at the same time bull trout were considered nuisance fish by most anglers, greedy cannibals who preyed on the more desirable rainbow, brook and brown trout. The commonly accepted wisdom was that they were unsophisticated fish: too easy to catch, sluggish fighters once hooked and their flesh inferior to that of other species.

Ignorance and greed, consequently, had a lot to do with the loss of a great native trout from streams like Meadow Creek. Most of us assumed that one species of trout or char could pretty much replace another. If bull trout vanished, then, it would be no great loss because a more desirable species like rainbow or brook trout would fill in the gaps. We killed all the bull trout we could catch and looked forward to catching real trout on our next visit.

Bull trout, however, cannot be replaced. They are ecologically as different from brook or rainbow trout as they are from suckers. Their unique adaptations to western Alberta's running water ecosystems make them the only species that can consistently grow to trophy dimensions in streams that otherwise produce only mediocre specimens of other trout and char species.

Biologists studying small streams near Edson found that upwelling springs in headwater streams provided vital spawning habitat for big bull trout.

After hatching, young bull trout remained in the headwater streams for four or five years feeding on insects and living pretty much like the native rainbows with which they shared those creeks. Unlike the rainbows, however, as they approached maturity they slipped down-stream into the bigger waters of the McLeod River and began to feed on whitefish, suckers and other small fish. At that point, their growth increased dramatically; the McLeod, like most Alberta rivers, is capable of producing seven-kilogram bull trout.

The researchers' most startling discovery, however, was that female bull trout don't reach sexual maturity until they are 40 centimetres long. Other trout species spawn at less than half that size.

Under the fishing regulations of the day most bull trout were being killed and eaten before they could spawn for the first time, because they were being managed as if they were no different from other species.

In 1991 the province introduced new regulations reflecting the new knowledge. Anglers were required to release any bull trout less than 40 centimetres to allow females to reach maturity. It was a small step in the right direction.

Meanwhile, Alberta anglers were growing increasingly concerned about the loss of stocks of bull trout, cutthroats and other native species. Through the 1980s there was growing interest in catch-and-release fishing, especially for high quality fish in high quality environments.

Jim Stelfox, a provincial fisheries biologist, looked at the new understanding of bull trout ecology and changing angler preferences, and began to suspect that bull trout may be the key to turning unproductive reservoirs into trophy fisheries.

Southern Alberta has many irrigation and hydro power reservoirs that are plagued with fisheries management problems, according to Stelfox. Because of the way in which water engineers raise and lower reservoir levels, there is no stable shoreline zone in these water bodies. As a result there is very little usable habitat for rainbow, cutthroat or brook trout that rely on near-shore areas. On the other hand, the reservoirs are often crowded with suckers that can feed on the bottom, competing with trout for the same limited food supply.

Bull trout, unlike most other trout species, are aggressive fish-eaters. That means they don't rely as much on the shoreline zone. Suckers, rather than competing with bull trout, are their food supply. Restoring bull trout populations may yield far more than continuing to pour expensive hatchery rainbows and brookies into reservoirs.

Lower Kananaskis Lake is a case in point. When bull trout were protected in this hydro power reservoir, populations rebounded dramatically. For the first decade after the closure, spawning numbers more than doubled annually. Even more remarkable is the fact that those spawners gained up to a kilogram each year, thanks to abundant suckers in the reservoir. One researcher caught the same female bull trout on a fly three times in the same week and in spite of the stress, she managed to spawn successfully and return the following year, having gained half a kilogram in weight, to be caught and released again.

"If you set out to design a fish for tourism," wrote Kyle McNeilly in Environment Views, "You'd come up with the bull trout. Bull trout grow to be large. You can see and watch them, especially during their spawning runs. You can catch them fairly easily and they release well. I've never met a tougher, more recyclable trout species."

In January 1993, a group of concerned anglers, biologists, fisheries managers and conservationists decided to form the Alberta Bull Trout Task Force. They agreed to collaborate on a recovery and management plan for the province. First they needed information, however, so they organized an international conference where experts in fish ecology could share recent research results and management experience.

The task force couldn't have timed things better. Their May 1994 conference coincided with the completion of numerous studies in the western U.S., most triggered by an earlier proposal to list the bull trout as an endangered species under U.S. law. Almost 200 delegates turned up.

Conference speakers revealed many reasons why bull trout are in trouble today. Road building associated with logging and energy development damages headwater streams, clogging once-clean gravels with silt and changing the timing and severity of floods. In some areas, including many parts of Alberta's forest reserves, poorly managed cattle grazing results in similar damage. Hybridization with introduced brook trout and competition with lake trout have eliminated some populations. Alberta's Ghost, Brazeau, Waterton and Oldman River dams are among many that have devastated migratory stocks, isolating unproductive headwaters populations from the productive lower river reaches that are vital to this late-maturing species.

But one common thread was found to apply in almost all areas. We have killed, and continue to kill, far too many bull trout.

Where bull trout populations were protected by restrictive fishing regulations, some spectacular angling has resulted. Lake Billy Chinook, a large reservoir in Oregon's DeChutes River system, is one success story There, a one-fish limit was instituted and anglers were encouraged to treat bull trout as a trophy fishery. Bull trout populations rebounded and fish in the nine-kilogram class are now common. Early results from Lower Kananaskis Lake reservoir, which was closed to bull trout harvest two years ago, seem to offer Albertans a similar prospect.

Brian Evans, then Alberta's Minister of Environment, took advantage of the conference to announce a new Bull Trout Management Plan for Alberta. Regulation changes in 1995 were proof of the province's long-overdue determination to bring back a great native fish.

Those of us who grew up with the myth of abundance might be excused for being frustrated by yet more restrictions on our angling. On the other hand, by learning to identify bull trout and teaching our children to turn them back, we can be part of a visionary conservation effort: restoring a unique species we helped endanger. Bull trout got into trouble one hook at a time; they can be brought back the same way.

Not long ago most anglers considered the bull trout a frontier fish whose time was past. New biological knowledge, new regulations and a new spirit of determination have turned all that around; the bull trout is the trophy fish of Alberta's future.

I had a glimpse of that future one recent fall day, on a small creek in southwestern Alberta. The fishery had fallen into dark days by the early 1980s because of a tradition by local anglers of travelling by horseback to the stream's headwaters each fall to kill the big spawners.

Just as conservationists began to talk gloomily of another bull trout disaster, a pine beetle infestation swept through the valley, killing most of its old lodgepole pines. The trail to the headwaters eventually became impassable for horses, a jackstraw tangle of down timber.

I set off to see whether bull trout numbers might be recovering, now that the trail was blocked. Two hours in I saw my first submarine: a vast, orange-sided bull trout that hung, heavy with spawn, above the multi-coloured stream bed. A slightly smaller male tended her.

A little farther upstream I found a pool full of elongated shadows. Ten huge bull trout lay on the bottom, like sunken cordwood, occasionally swirling to chase one another before returning to their positions, head into the current. For the next couple of kilometres of stream I found one spawning redd after another, including an immense redd that appeared unoccupied until a 75-centimetre female suddenly churned her way upstream out of a riffle and slid quietly into the backwater beneath my feet.

She held her position against the pulsing surge of newborn waters, gills opening and closing, oblivious to me, obeying an ancient imperative that had guided her kind to these same headwaters for millennia. Standing centimetres away, I looked about at the wild valley and its quiet little stream.

Something began to swell inside me as I listened to the quiet babble of living water, watched the clouds seething past silent peaks and looked down at the great fish swaying in the current. This stream could have been Meadow or Johnston Creek or any of the streams of my youth-streams I thought I knew well. But I hadn't known them, because only now was I seeing how they really could have been, how they used to be; how they were meant to be. I ached with realization; I wanted to scream aloud.

We treated bull trout like vermin, and in our ignorance robbed ourselves of the opportunity to know the full reality of western Alberta's cold-water ecosystems. All those creeks, all those places, were only pale shadows of what they could have been, because in our ignorance and our lack of humility we took away the great golden bull trout that belong there. How could we have been so wrong?

But that was then and this is now, and although some bull trout fisheries have been lost forever, others wait only for human restraint to restore them to what they were and again can be. It is a new century, and the dark days are behind for a fish that deserved better.

The bull trout is native to Alberta's cold-water ecosystems, part of our shared heritage and, now, part of our common future. In that future, anglers will again see submarines in tiny headwater streams. In that future, bull trout will no longer be the stuff of myth and misunderstanding.

In that future a great native fish will again be a part of how we know our streams, our home places and ourselves.

Fish Without Hooks

 A large spring bubbles from the base of a cliff just a few kilometres northeast of the town of Jasper. It piles up in a clear pool full of filamentous green algae and sunken logs then slides silkily into a culvert to pass beneath the Yellowhead Highway. Emerging from the culvert as a shallow, gravel-bottomed creek, it flows 100 metres to lose itself in the silt-grey waters of the Athabasca River.

Each May, park warden Bill Hunt surveys the backwater where the creek joins the river. Bill has a special interest in harlequin ducks. Most days he finds two or three pairs of these unique little ducks bobbing in the current and diving to hunt along the gravel bottom.

A short walk down from the highway reveals the source of the harlequin ducks' bounty. Step close to the creek and, mirage-like, a whole segment of the creek bed swirls away in a striated mass of orange and grey then stabilizes again in deep water. Look more closely, and there are the suckers: hundreds of brightly coloured fish stacked like cordwood along the creek bed.

Long-nosed suckers are common in Alberta's lakes and rivers, including the glacially cold and silt-clouded waters of the Athabasca River. Like the six other sucker species found in the province, long-nosed suckers spend most of their lives foraging in the bottom sediment, rooting out the larvae of small insects, worms and other invertebrates.

Each year after the ice goes out and the spring sun begins to warm the water, the lengthening days trigger a shift in the sucker's habits. Taking on bright spawning colours—the males are particularly striking with black and red stripes down each side—the suckers crowd together and begin to forge upstream. Following subtle scents and chemical traces in the swirling currents, they arrive, at length, on their spawning grounds in gravel-bottomed tributaries. There each female releases up to 20,000 eggs into the current.

Nature only requires that each female replace herself with one or two others; the rest of those eggs are surplus. Tumbling along the riverbed, some are attacked by bacteria and fungi that in turn will become food for small invertebrates. Others become food for trout and other fish. And some get eaten by harlequin ducks.

"Alberta's harlequin ducks are at the eastern edge of the species' range," says Bill Hunt, explaining why park authorities are so interested in them. "We know they're very loyal to their home ranges, but we really don't know very much about their ecology."

Jasper's interest in harlequin ducks came about when a dramatic increase in commercial rafting on the Maligne River was found to coincide with a dramatic drop in use of that river by harlequin ducks. It was in the course of trying to learn more about a duck that nests in turbulent mountain rivers that researchers found the link between harlequin ducks and suckers.

Harlequin ducks winter in the intertidal zone along the edge of the Pacific Ocean before following the thaw back to their headwaters breeding grounds. Arriving in Alberta, the ducks face an ecological dilemma; they have just used up a great deal of energy in migration, the females will soon face the rigours of laying and incubating eggs and mountain streams produce very little food. How fortuitous, then, that spawning suckers should choose just that critical season to crowd into tributary streams; few food sources are as energy-rich as fish spawn.

White suckers, too, spawn in May. As the ice comes off higher-elevation streams, other fish species like rainbow trout begin to spawn. By the time the female harlequin ducks are ready to nest, they have enjoyed several weeks of high-protein feeding and are ready for the rigours of incubation.

When I was young I knew about suckers. They were trash fish. Other anglers told me that they ate trout eggs and competed with useful fish for food. If you caught one when fishing for trout or whitefish, the expected thing to do was to throw it back in the bushes to die. One less trash fish to clutter up the river.

Now that I'm older and a bit wiser, I know that a harlequin duck would likely disagree with so narrow a view. So, too, would a northern pike, an otter or a black bear, only a few of the many species of wildlife that rely, in part, on the uniquely adapted sucker as part of their diet.

Alberta's streams and lakes harbour more than 50 species of native fishes. Most are unknown even to those of us who call ourselves fishermen and think we know something about fish. From tiny arctic lampreys twisting their way upstream through the Slave River rapids to spawn below Mountain Rapids, to brown stonecats feeling their way along the bottom of the muddy Milk River, Alberta's diversity of fishes reflects the diversity of our aquatic environments. Each species of fish is linked through ecological processes and food webs to everything else, ultimately, in its watershed.

The natural rhythms and cycles of the streams and lakes define the nature of existence for fish that live in their waters. Just as the lengthening days of spring combine with a slow increase in water temperature to signal spawning season to suckers, so does each fish population integrate its existence with the predictable variations of its environment.

Where does the ecosystem end and the fish begin? Ultimately, of course, all are one.

Consider southern Alberta's prairie rivers, for example. Unlike the cool, forested landscapes through which the Athabasca River flows, southern rivers like the lower Bow, Oldman and Milk rivers carve their way through a dry landscape whose natural vegetation is shortgrass prairie. With little vegetation to protect the soil from heavy rains, prairie rivers carry heavy loads of silt much of the year. In addition, they flood each May and June, when snowmelt in their mountain headwaters corresponds with the annual peak in rainfall.

Big spring floods of silty water are a normal part of the annual cycle along prairie rivers—not a natural disaster, but an essential part of river ecology.

The forests that grow along the floodplains of prairie rivers are adapted to spring floods. Indeed, cottonwoods and sandbar willows need floods for their very survival. Even though June floods tend to wash out a lot of the old trees, they also deposit fresh mud and silt on shallow parts of the floodplains and on point bars just at the season when cottonwoods release billions of fluffy white seeds. The seeds take root on the new silt. Irrigated by next spring's floods, they soon get their roots down into the water table, and a new generation of trees spread their leaves under the prairie sun.

Along the rims of new midstream islands and sandbars, dense clusters of young sandbar willows raise their narrow, shiny leaves into the same sunlight, having been born of the same coincidence of rain, snowmelt, silt, erosion and deposition.

All those leaves are the key to much of the river's productivity. In a grassland environment, one of the single most important sources of vegetable matter to nurture the river ecosystem is the leaves shed each fall from the golden galleries of cottonwoods lining the river. Blown on the prairie wind, many of the leaves light at last on the surface of the shrunken river where they grow waterlogged and sink, to lodge in quiet riffles and backwaters.

Through the long fall and winter, the leaves feed a rich diversity of fungi, bacteria, protozoa and invertebrates. Caddis larvae, mayfly nymphs, aquatic worms: a host of small life forms thrive on the annual harvest of leaves from floodplain forests.

The Iowa darter is a tiny relative of the better-known northern pike. Along with shorthead sculpin, brook stickleback, long-nosed dace, lake chub and other small fishes, darters forage along the bottom of the Milk River and in the shallows along the shoreline, feeding on the abundance of invertebrates and other animals that process the leaf litter. The larger stonecat, Alberta's only member of the catfish family, shares in the feast but also, from time to time, catches and eats the small fish species. Burbot, a species of cod that hunts at night with the aid of sensitive barbels that protrude whisker-like from the sides of its face, hunt the smaller fishes, as do sauger and other predatory species. The food chain extends back from the water into floodplain forests where common mergansers and raccoons, which feed on the small fishes that abound in the silty shallows, raise their young each year in the hollow trunks of old cottonwoods. Excreting the nitrogen-rich remains of digested fish, these terrestrial predators fertilize riparian thickets with their droppings. And so the river and its surroundings, again, become one thing through the alchemy of fishes.

Just as floodplain forests are married to the natural rhythms of large rivers, so are the life cycles of the fishes that dwell there. Some species find themselves stimulated to spawn by the predictable rise in water levels that coincides with spring floods, or the increasing light saturation of early summer as silty floodwaters give way to the clearer flows of summer. Brook sticklebacks, for example, spawn during the same spring floods that sustain the cottonwood trees whose leaves help feed them. The tiny fishes migrate into seasonally flooded ponds or even into flooded fields where males build tiny nests of vegetation debris and algae. The adults jealously guard their nests, attached to sedge stems or other rooted material, until the eggs hatch and the young disperse.

Although prairie rivers may sometimes intimidate anglers with their size and heavy, silt-laden flow, the diversity of their fish populations is far greater than that of the better-known foothills trout streams. From the tiny trout perch and sticklebacks to the two-metre lake sturgeon, as many as 30 different species occur in the South Saskatchewan River, for example, compared with fewer than 15 in the rivers and streams of Banff National Park. Abundant populations of fish-eating predators such as white pelicans, cormorants, mergansers and mink reflect the productivity of eastern Alberta's large rivers.

Just as rivers respond in predictable ways to natural cycles and changes taking place in their watersheds, so do lakes. Spring floodwaters raise lake levels and bring a flush of nutrients from the surrounding landscape. Summer sun heats the lake water and contributes to an increase in production of algae and other plants. In winter, most Alberta lakes are ice-covered.

Fish that occupy lakes enjoy a more stable environment than those in streams; they need not adjust to changes in flow rates and much of the vegetable matter that forms the foundation of their food chains grows right in the lake, rather than being imported through leaf-fall. They also face their own unique set of ecological challenges, however. For instance, oxygen supply can drop dramatically in summer when algae populations explode, using up most of the available oxygen. Winter can also be a time of oxygen loss since ice-covered lakes are isolated from the air above, and snow on the ice blocks the sunlight aquatic vegetation needs to manufacture oxygen underwater. Temperature changes can be stressful too, especially in midsummer when stationary water bodies absorb heat dramatically.

Fishes respond in various ways. Lake whitefish and walleye adjust their positions in the water column to find the most comfortable temperatures; in midsummer they usually feed at greater depths than in winter. Many lake species can tolerate low oxygen for short periods, but in lakes where oxygen levels repeatedly fall to very low levels, only a few of the most tolerant species like lake chub survive.

Each lake or stream is a unique and complex ecosystem. Each is the result of centuries of evolution, intimately connected to the forests, meadows and landscapes that define its watershed. The chemistry of the water, its annual flood cycle, predictable changes in oxygen level, water temperature and organic enrichment: each ecological feature of its watershed shapes, ultimately, the nature of that water body.

A river or lake, by its very nature, lies at the bottom of a watershed. Everything that happens in that watershed expresses itself, ultimately, in the behaviour or health of that river or lake. Log a forest, spill a pollutant or pave a road, and the results will show up downstream. Rivers whose headwaters have been heavily logged experience more pronounced spring floods without the forests to hold back the waters, and also suffer more pronounced summer droughts. Contaminants dumped into coulees or spilled into the soil eventually find their way into groundwater or runoff and turn up in nearby lakes.

Fishes live in those lakes and rivers: immersed, inseparable, utterly integrated.

Change the natural rhythms of a river or a lake, or contaminate it with toxins, nutrients or heat, and the fishes that dwell there have no choice but to respond. Fishes feed on insects, worms and other forms of aquatic life, so they accumulate any toxins that find their way into the body tissues of those prey species. The life cycles of fishes are tied to the natural cycles of the water bodies where they live. When water temperatures reach a certain level, or when spring floods change the depth, speed and clarity of water, fishes respond in ways that have evolved over the centuries. They are utterly at the mercy of any changes or damage to their watersheds, because they live in water, the heart of every ecosystem.

Break the ecological webs that sustain the populations of Alberta's diverse and little-known fish populations, and the consequences may be hard to predict; Jasper's harlequin ducks offer a hint of the subtle, but essential, connections among fishes and other elements of their ecosystems.

Most of our knowledge of fishes derives from the desire to catch and eat them. It may be, however, as we strive to find ways to measure sustainability and to understand the ecosystems that sustain us all, that it will be the fish without hooks that teach us the most useful lessons about the threads that bind all of us, ultimately, to the living waters that flow from the landscapes our choices shape.

Ghost Forests

It's usually late spring before you can hike in to Forum Lake. Tucked up against the base of cliffs that form part of the Continental Divide, ice often blankets the lake well into late June. Its cirque faces northeast, sheltered from the high-elevation sun. Snowdrifts linger in the shady timberline forests well into July most years.

Morning mist tangles the treetops and drifts in shredded tatters along the walls of ancient rock that loom above the lake. Wraithlike and jagged, the whitened spars of dead trees rise high above the darker canopy of fir trees. Varied thrushes whistle eerily. A raven croaks. Later the sun will break through and burn a brave brightness into the mountain morning, but for now the timberline basin feels like a place of ghosts.

It *is* a place of ghosts. Bleached arms bent, dead whitebark pines stand mute and still, lifeless reminders of a time not long past when this basin echoed to the rasping cries of Clark's nutcrackers and the chatter of red squirrels. Most of the timberline giants have died over the past half century, starving the subalpine forest of its annual bounty of oil-rich pine seeds. A century ago, grizzly bears followed their noses from one squirrel midden to another in this part of the Canadian Rockies, raiding the treasure troves of whitebark seeds. Today's squirrel middens contain a more trivial bounty of fir, spruce and lodgepole cones; today's grizzlies have to make do with other foods. In Yellowstone and Jasper national parks where whitebark pine stands have yet to suffer the fate of Forum Lake's whitebarks, bears still rob squirrels.

Hike to timberline anywhere in the Rocky Mountains along the 49th parallel and the same picturesque ghost forests of whitebark pine snags will greet you. To those who don't know the story behind the dead trees, they seem to speak of little more than the difficulty of life up high near timberline. To those who know why the spectacular high mountain pine trees are dying out, however, the dead snags are mute testimony to the dark side of 20th century conservation.

"Whitebark and limber pine forests are functionally extinct in the Waterton-Glacier International Peace Park," says American ecologist Kate Kendall. With biologists from Parks Canada, the U.S. Forest Service and other agencies responsible for managing the pines' high-country habitats, Kate Kendall has studied the ongoing die-off of one of the most spectacular, and ecologically important, of Rocky Mountain trees. Now, in what seems to some like a desperate race against time, she is working with those same colleagues to help the trees save themselves.

Unlike the better-known lodgepole, jack and Ponderosa pines, the whitebark (*Pinus albicaulis*) and its lower-elevation relative the limber pine (*Pinus flexilis*) are members of the stone pine group. They bear their needles in bunches of five and produce large cones with nutlike seeds the size of a cherry pit. Stone pines are circumboreal, with several species in Europe and Asia. Most grow in semi-arid environments, often on rocky ridges and outcrops, where their deep roots and drought-resistant needles enable them to cope with limited water supplies. Although few other trees can compete with these specialized pines in their rugged habitats, the frequent fires that are a natural feature of dry landscapes help reduce competition further by burning up seedlings of upstart fir or spruce trees. Stone pines have fire-resistant bark and, by using up the available water near them, minimize the grasses and other fine fuels next to their trunks.

Perhaps the most remarkable aspect of stone pine ecology is the interdependent relationship between the trees and nutcrackers-curve-billed members of the crow family. Whitebarks and limber pines are synonymous with Clark's nutcracker, a raucous and sociable black-and-grey bird somewhat smaller than a crow. Nutcrackers rely on energy-rich pine seeds to feed their offspring. Since cone crops vary in productivity from one year to the next, however, the birds need to hedge their bets by gathering pine seeds when they are abundant and hiding them for later retrieval when they may be scarce.

Nutcrackers use their stout beaks to pry seeds out of pine cones. Tilting its head up, a nutcracker will stash each seed in its gular pouch-a hollowed-out space beneath its tongue. Once it has five to 10 seeds, it flies to an open slope up to several hundred metres away, lands on the ground, pokes a beak-length hole in the ground and empties its gular pouch into the hole. A couple of quick pokes and the hole is covered. Calling sociably as they flock back and forth between treetops and caching sites, flocks of nutcrackers work compulsively for hours on end.

Diana Tombeck, an ecology professor at the University of Colorado, studied nutcracker food-caching behaviour as part of her PhD studies. She estimated that an individual nutcracker might gather and store up to 90,000 seeds in a single summer. Experimenting with captive birds, she found that their spatial memory is nothing short of astounding. Using sticks, rocks and other markers as reference points, her study nutcrackers were unfailingly able to retrieve every seed they had cached. Only if researchers moved one of the markers did the birds fail to find their hidden food supplies.

Nutcrackers, however, are over-achievers. Their food-caching behaviour far exceeds the needs of the average nutcracker family. Of the 40,000 to 90,000 seeds each nutcracker hides it usually retrieves less than a third. Some of the rest are lost but many are simply abandoned.

Pine seeds are critical food for nutcracker nestlings. The birds retrieve enough seeds to ensure the survival of the next nutcracker generation. The seeds that remain behind, however, ensure the next generation of pines. Each stash of seeds is at the ideal depth for germination. Because nutcrackers choose sunny, open slopes—they particularly favour recently burned sites—the sprouting seedlings enjoy abundant sun and little competition from other plants. The relationship between nutcracker and pine, in other words, works to the advantage of both parties: a classic symbiotic relationship.

It's a relationship that's in trouble, however, partly due to the misguided enthusiasm of North America's early forest conservationists.

During the early years of the 20th century, Americans became concerned about the rate at which timber barons were devastating that nation's forests. President Theodore Roosevelt established national forests to protect what remained and hired Gifford Pinchot as the first head of the U.S. Forest Service. Pinchot, a staunch believer in conservation-the philosophy of wise use of natural resources-set about to change the way American forestry was done. In Canada, Prime Minister Wilfred Laurier organized several forestry congresses to promote a similar change in management philosophy for our forest estate. Gifford Pinchot was an honoured guest at the first Canadian Forestry Congress in 1906.

Among the changes to forest management that arose on both sides of the border with the establishment of public forests and forest management agencies, was a move to improve the quality of North American trees. Pinchot and others felt that North American forests were little better than raw materials, sorely in need of improvement through management. Selective breeding and progressive techniques of forest culture were among the ways foresters determined to improve native forests. Since some of the best available silvicultural expertise of the day was in Germany, scientists in Pinchot's agency shipped seeds and seedlings of North American trees overseas to be improved by selective breeding in German plantations. Among the species that went to Europe were eastern and western white pines-five-needle pines that, unlike the related limber and whitebark pines, produce high-quality lumber.

When the "improved" trees came back to North America they brought a hitchhiker: white pine blister rust. Blister rust is endemic to Europe, where pine trees long ago developed resistance to its ravages. North America's five-needle pines, however, had never been exposed to the fungal disease. With no built-in resistance, our native trees were, and are, extremely vulnerable to infection. Ironically, scientific forestry in the service of wise use proved more devastating to North America's five needle pine forests than the ravages of the 19th century's unbridled commercial exploitation. Eastern white pine forests have yet to recover from the combined devastation of overcutting and blister rust. Only an aggressive breeding program to select for rust-resistance has saved western white pine forests from vanishing.

The commercial value of the white pines at least motivated foresters to try and undo the harm they had unleashed on this continent. Lacking any economic value, however, wind-gnarled limber and whitebark pine forests were left to die. Death by blister rust is a slow, insidious process that begins with rust spores infecting a single branch then gradually killing that branch as the fungus spreads down the tree's vascular system to the trunk. Blister-like swellings girdle the trunk at the base of the infected branch, gradually killing the top of the tree. After several years, the tree finally dies completely. Since slow-growing whitebark pines may be 100 years old before they produce their first cone, the disease often kills trees before they get a chance to reproduce.

Gnarled and scenic, the growing number of dead snags up near timberline went unnoticed for many years because the attention of foresters was focused on economically productive forests farther downslope. A third of all the whitebark and limber pines in the Waterton-Glacier International Peace Park were already dead before Kate Kendall and her research associates began to investigate the problem in the late 1990s. More disturbing yet, from half to almost 95 percent of trees in the surviving stands were infected with blister rust and, consequently, doomed to early death.

Blister rust has been in western forests for almost a century. Its spread has been uneven. While the worst damage is concentrated along the 49th parallel in a fan-shaped area extending from near Vancouver to the Waterton-Glacier International Peace Park, whitebark pine forests farther north and south have yet to show much sign of damage. In Jasper National Park, flocks of nutcrackers greet tourists at the base of Mount Edith Cavell; on the slopes above, the rounded tops of healthy whitebark pines dominate a forest that shows no sign of infection. Yellowstone National Park is similarly healthy, although early signs of blister rust infestation have ecologists there worried. Yellowstone's endangered grizzly bears rely on whitebark pine nuts scavenged from squirrel middens for critical summer food. If blister rust devastates Yellowstone's whitebark forests—likely, if global climate change brings a predicted increase in summer humidity—ecologists fear the ecosystem's capacity to support grizzly bears will be drastically reduced.

Nobody knows whether whitebark pines were once as important a bear food in the more badly infected regions along the 49th parallel.

Two mid-century biologists reported sign of grizzlies feeding on pine nuts. During her 1997 field investigations in Waterton Kate Kendall found bear scats full of limber pine seeds. For the most part, however, whitebark stands were already suffering heavy mortality before anyone started asking questions about their role in Rocky Mountain ecology.

The late 20th century, belatedly, brought an awakening interest in non-commercial forest values among government agencies and conservation groups. A heavily attended 1987 conference in Missoula, Montana drew forest experts from numerous agencies and universities together to plan strategies for saving the threatened whitebark ecosystem.

What's needed, all agreed, is for whitebark pine populations to be given the chance to develop rust resistance. Some agencies like the U.S. Forest Service and B.C. Ministry of Forests have selective breeding facilities that they have used, in the past, to develop disease-resistant strains in other western trees. At least in the U.S., whitebark pine breeding programs are already under way. The problem with growing rust-resistant seedlings in nurseries, however, is that many die when planted back into natural habitats. Given the sheer geographical scale of the problem, selective breeding is unlikely to make a big impact.

Canadian and U.S. national parks, unlike neighbouring multiple-use agencies, are mandated to work with natural ecological processes. Park vegetation specialists in both countries are now looking to prescribed fire as a way to kick-start natural selection for rust resistance. They point out that if it weren't for aggressive fire control programs, lightning strikes would have maintained a mosaic of various-aged forests at timberline through the 20th century, rather than the aging stands that dominate today. Without frequent fires, subalpine fir and other shade-tolerant trees eventually crowd out the sun-loving whitebarks and, ironically, expose them to the risk of death from much more intense fires fuelled by the dense foliage of the ingrown forests.

The least rust-resistant whitebark pines in most stands are already dead. Although nutcrackers stash seeds from those that have survived the 20th century, mortality among pine seedlings is high in the timberline environment. Only on recently burned slopes where conditions are ideal for regeneration do high numbers of pine seedlings successfully sprout and grow. For vegetation ecologists like Kate Kendall and Kootenay National Park's Rob Walker, small burned patches offer the best hope of filling the mountain landscape with young whitebark pines. All of those, inevitably, will be exposed to blister rust spores. Most ultimately will die. Those whose genetic makeup keeps them immune to rust attack, however, will grow and, in a few decades, begin to produce new generations of pines with increasingly high rates of rust resistance.

The key is to get lots of young whitebarks growing while the dwindling supply of old whitebarks are still producing enough seed. And the challenge is getting the okay to set fires in scenic, high-elevation forests. Land use managers are understandably timid about letting their staff start forest fires that might upset a public brainwashed by Smokey the Bear. Even more worrisome is the thought that some fires could escape and burn neighbouring commercial forests, farmlands or other property.

Rob Walker feels there is little cause for nervousness with well-planned prescribed burns. He conducted Canada's only whitebark pine restoration burn to date. The 12-hectare prescribed fire near the Crowfoot Glacier in Banff National Park went off flawlessly in October 1998. "We know it was an intense fire," says Walker. "We got 100 percent crown scorch and more than 70 percent organic soil loss. Monitoring so far shows excellent herbaceous regeneration. We won't know how well we met our pine objectives until we get a good cone crop year and that hasn't happened yet."

Farther south, forest managers in the Bitterroot National Forest near Missoula, Montana have already found prolific whitebark pine restoration in experimental units they burned in the mid-1990s. Rob Walker is planning a larger fire in Yoho National Park's isolated Sodalite Creek valley and his colleagues in other Rocky Mountain parks have similar plans on the books.

"One thing that works in our favour that I hadn't originally anticipated," says Walker "is how dry the sites actually are. You think of them as cool and damp because they're at timberline but they're usually quite well-drained. The other thing is that we have our choice of many topographically isolated sites where talus and rock can be used to keep the fires from spreading."

Some British Columbia forestry companies have recently shown an interest in working with the B.C. Ministry of Forests to restore whitebark pine stands there. Most whitebarks grow above the operability line-the elevation contour where it is uneconomic to log. Even so, logging companies often use fire to get rid of logging slash in cutblocks just downslope from whitebark stands. Late fall slash burns deliberately designed to burn upslope into whitebark pine stands could be valuable for creating patchwork openings full of young, regenerating pine trees. Given the role that commercial forestry considerations played in unleashing the blister rust problem, there is a kind of symmetry to the idea that commercial forest companies might have a role to play in undoing some of the harm.

The silent snags reflected in Forum Lake's icy waters stand as silent reproof to the hasty arrogance of early forest conservationists, and a continuing challenge to the current generation. Twentieth-century forest management resulted in the slow, insidious devastation of an entire forest ecosystem. If 21st-century forest management fails to reverse that decline, the price of that failure will be measured in Clark's nutcrackers, squirrels, grizzly bears and the spreading silence of those high-mountain ghost forests. It is a haunting challenge.

Maligned Ducks

The headwater streams and rivers are still ice-covered when the first harlequin ducks wing their way in from the Pacific coast late in April. The harlequin ducks appear as if by magic one morning, on the open channels of the Athabasca River. While the mountain spring spreads up the valleys through the following weeks, the strikingly marked ducks feed in shallow riffles or bask on the edges of small islands, courting and breeding as they wait for the spring thaw to open up the high country.

By mid-May the Athabasca is turning brown from snowmelt and spring rains. Unlike its tributaries, the Maligne River remains relatively clear. The lower reach of the river is almost entirely spring-fed in early spring. Farther upstream, the reach of river connecting world-renowned Maligne Lake with Medicine Lake also remains clear because Maligne Lake, one of the largest lakes in the Canadian Rockies, acts as a huge settling pond for silt washed down from the glaciers that form its headwaters.

By mid-June the harlequins have dispersed upstream from the Athabasca to seek out nest sites along the Maligne and other headwater streams. Most—usually 20 or so—remain near the outlet of Maligne Lake where abundant invertebrates and, later in the spring, the eggs of spawning rainbow trout provide a rich food supply. Late in June the males migrate west again, across the Rockies and back to the rocky intertidal zones of the Pacific Ocean. Left behind, the females raise their young in the most unlikely of duck habitats: icy, brawling streams that tumble out of alpine valleys.

Unlike the endangered eastern population, up to 200,000 harlequin ducks remain scattered across their traditional western range in the mountains from Wyoming and Washington north through Alaska into eastern Asia.

Even so, harlequin ducks are common only on their wintering

grounds and a few spring staging areas along major Rocky Mountain rivers. A hard summer day's searching will rarely turn up more than one or two families of young harlequins. Mountain rivers, because of their short ice-free season, volatile flow and cold temperatures, are among the least productive aquatic ecosystems in Canada, sustaining low densities of both invertebrates and animals that feed on them. Jasper National Park's streams are fed by glacial meltwaters that keep them cold and silty, further reducing their biological productivity.

The Maligne is one exception. Until very recently, the 15 kilometres of river between Maligne and Medicine lakes supported at least 11 breeding pairs of harlequin duck-an exceptionally high density of nearly one pair per kilometre. By contrast, the highest recorded density of the endangered eastern harlequin duck populations of Labrador and the James Bay watersheds is only one pair per 10 kilometres.

Where the Maligne River escapes from Maligne Lake, birders enjoy access to one of the most easily observed populations of harlequin ducks in North America. A bridge across the outlet gives easy views of brightly coloured males courting their mates and foraging in the rapids from mid-May through early July. The outlet stream's water is so clear that watchers can even see the ducks foraging among the cobbles and gravel of the river bottom. A rich supply of stoneflies, mayflies, caddis and, in June, trout eggs makes this site exceptionally valuable for females who need to build up their energy levels for the nesting season, and for both sexes before the fall migration back to the Pacific.

Jasper National Park warden Peter Clarkson compiled a status report on the park's harlequin ducks in 1992. He concluded that the Maligne offers exceptional habitat because the river is a clean, relatively stable, whitewater stream: ideal habitat for harlequin ducks—and for river rafters.

One morning in June 1986 I joined a group of adventurous souls at the Maligne Lake teahouse where we were issued wet suits and paddles and ushered down to the lakeshore by our Maligne River Adventure guides. Three new rubber rafts were pulled up on the gravel. Just a few metres away, lines of smooth current showed beneath the bridge. Four harlequin ducks were diving in the outlet channel.

Once we had mastered the basic paddle strokes the rafts turned and, one by one, slipped into the current. The ducks flushed out onto the lake as we drew near. Ahead, the river dropped from sight and growing thunder warned us of what was coming.

From Maligne Lake the river drops fast—over 10 metres in the first two kilometres—almost twice the maximum drop of the Colorado River in the Grand Canyon. The Express, as rafters call this reach, is a chaos of white, foaming holes, glassy standing waves and roaring walls of blue water. Guides shouted instructions and steered us expertly past huge boulders. My companions and I laughed and yelled as waves repeatedly crashed over us, our voices promptly swallowed by the thunder of water.

Then the river tipped back to a more reasonable angle and the rest of the trip became a series of short floats over clean gravel interrupted by sudden descents into chaos. Eleven kilometres downstream we eddied into a powerful backwater and escaped to dry land, exhilarated and soaked. A waiting van hauled passengers and rafts back to Maligne Lake, where another party was already waiting at the launch site.

I've paddled many western Canadian rivers, and rafted a few others, but never have I had such a perfect whitewater float as on the Maligne— a small, intimate river in pristine surroundings, clean, full of exhilarating rapids and surrounded with some of the finest scenery in the world.

Others feel the same way. The popularity of the Maligne River among commercial rafting companies skyrocketed in the years following my 1986 adventure. By the mid-1990s three commercial raft companies were operating on the river. The number of raft trips increased from six in 1986—the year I floated the river—to well over 2,000 per summer only a few years later. As word got out, kayaking and private rafting use increased too.

The entire Maligne River watershed is in Jasper National Park. As a national park, Jasper is required to make ecological integrity the first priority in planning for visitor use. However, the radical growth in the popularity of the Maligne River for outfitted rafting groups was totally unplanned. In fact, the Parks Service conducted only one cursory environmental impact assessment for only one of the three operations using the river. Park authorities were caught unawares by the explosion of interest in a river that had previously been considered too wild to appeal to boaters. As a result, during those first few years, management of human use of this unique ecosystem appeared to involve little more than rubber-stamping business licences in the Park administration office.

Volcker Schelhas immigrated to Canada from Germany in the late 1970s. In 1984 he moved to Jasper National Park and became manager of the Maligne Canyon Hostel.

Volcker had looked in vain for harlequin ducks in Europe, where the species occurs only along parts of the Atlantic coast in winter. When he finally arrived in Jasper, he discovered the ducks that so fascinated him virtually in his backyard.

Curious to learn more, Volcker began a series of regular annual censuses of harlequin ducks on the Maligne Lake outlet and parts of the Maligne River from May through July. In 1990 he wrote a concerned letter to the Park Superintendent after his data began to show a decline in sightings of harlequin ducks on the river, coinciding with the rapid growth in raft traffic. Volcker's letter came at a critical time.

Even as growing crowds of rafters were discovering the Maligne River, legislative changes were in the works to strengthen Canada's National Parks Act. Parks Canada has always been mandated to manage recreational use in ways that would keep national parks unimpaired for future generations. Not everyone agreed on what "unimpaired" meant, however, so in 1988 Bill C-30 made "ecological integrity through the protection of natural resources" the paramount legal requirement in visitor use and park zoning. Major Supreme Court decisions around the same time had made it clear to federal officials that they had better start taking their environmental responsibilities more seriously. Then, in 1992, environmentalists won a landmark court case ending commercial logging in Wood Buffalo National Park and making it plain, once and for all, that ecosystem protection must come first in Canada's national parks.

In 1991 the Jasper warden service assigned Peter Clarkson to study the declining harlequin ducks. He conducted an exhaustive literature review, surveyed park rivers to count breeding pairs and coordinated observation studies of harlequin ducks on the Maligne River through the rafting season. One treasure trove of data proved to be Volcker's personal study, which spanned the previous six years. In addition, some of the raft guides from Maligne River Adventures volunteered to document the responses of harlequin ducks to passing rafts.

Clarkson learned that harlequin duck counts on the Maligne had declined by up to 75 percent from the mid-1980s to the early 1990s. More than half of all ducks whose reactions to passing rafts were recorded flushed and flew away. Some females spent up to half an hour on Maligne Lake before returning to the river to resume feeding; time they could ill afford to waste. Observers reported no harlequin duck broods along the rafted portion of the river.

Clarkson conceded that factors other than just recreational rafting were likely implicated in the apparent loss of Maligne River harlequin ducks. The Exxon Valdez oil spill, for example, took a heavy toll on Alaskan harlequin ducks on their wintering grounds; no doubt smaller oil spills that chronically plague the whole Pacific coast kill others. A late spring in 1991 may have changed the dispersal patterns of ducks into the headwaters. The study's sample sizes were too small to draw confident statistical conclusions.

Nonetheless, U.S. biologists had already identified recreational use of rivers as a major threat to harlequin duck populations in each of the seven states they occupy. A 1993 multi-agency report on the status of harlequin ducks in North America revealed that populations in Oregon's southern Cascade and Wallowa Mountains were now extirpated. It also noted that harlequins had decreased significantly along Washington's Methow River because of increasingly heavy recreational use.

Of all the factors that might be causing harlequin ducks to avoid the Maligne, only one was under the direct control of Parks Canada: human use of the ducks' breeding and staging habitat. Clarkson recommended that commercial rafting be prohibited on the middle Maligne River during the critical spring staging period. It was not what the rafting company operators wanted to hear.

Mike Merilovich runs On-Line Tackle and Sports, a small business he built from scratch in Jasper. He sells fishing tackle and mountain biking gear. He also books rafting trips for the companies that specialize in literally immersing visiting tourists in nature.

Mike was sceptical about the need to protect the Maligne's harlequin ducks. "They aren't endangered," he said in a 1993 interview. "There's tens of thousands of those ducks west of here in B.C. Jasper's the very eastern edge of their range and anyway, there's lots of other rivers in the park where they can live completely undisturbed."

From Mike's point of view, Parks Canada caved in to pressure from environmental groups and solved a non-problem while ignoring bigger problems. "I've lived here 17 years," he said, "and suddenly Parks Canada wants to fix the environment. If they really wanted to do something for the environment they'd take a look early any summer morning when Maligne Tours fires up its diesel tour boats and the smog spreads across the lake. I've had to wipe globs of diesel fuel off my fishing lines down at Fisherman's Bay so many times and nothing gets done about that, but now they want to save some ducks that aren't even endangered!"

Volcker disagrees with Mike about the ducks, but he agrees about Parks Canada's inability to come to terms with ongoing environmental problems. Volcker needs only look across the road from his small hostel to the massive restaurant and gift shop built near the rim of Maligne Canyon in the early 1990s: more incremental tourism development in Jasper National Park's already heavily developed montane zone.

"Who started people coming here?" Merilovich asked. "Parks, that's who. They built the roads, they stocked the lakes with fish. I've invested hundreds of thousands of dollars in boats and inventory because Parks wanted tourists. But in 1984 they stopped stocking trout, now they're closing the Maligne River...What are they going to do, put a gate at the park entrance and just hand out pictures of the place?"

On the Maligne River, it appears, some of Parks Canada's crows have begun to come home to roost. A half century of political compromises, direct ecosystem manipulation and waffling on the incremental impacts of tourism development led local business people to expect continuing tourism investment opportunities. Now, with evolving public values, stronger legislation and legal precedent forcing Parks Canada to get serious about ecological restoration, the social and economic costs of necessary but belated changes are only starting to be tallied.

The science of conservation biology argues for applying what is known as the "precautionary principle" in making decisions about ecosystems. In short, this means that if there seems to be a problem but not enough information exists to be sure, the responsible approach is to assume there is until more study proves otherwise. Too often, the lack of definitive research has served as an excuse to keep on logging, or building or polluting while scientists conduct more expensive, inconclusive studies. This "innocent until proven guilty" approach to development has resulted in lasting harm to many wildlife populations and their habitats.

Jasper's park superintendent examined Clarkson's study, listened to groups like the Jasper Environmental Association and conservationists like Volker Schelhas, consulted with harlequin duck specialist Ian Goudie of the Canadian Wildlife Service, considered his duties under the amended National Parks Act and made an unprecedented decision: he chose to apply the precautionary principle.

In 1993, under the authority of Section 7(1) of the National Parks Act General Regulations, then-Superintendent Gaby Fortin closed the Maligne River to all human use between May 1 and July 1, to let the ducks settle in, breed and start incubating eggs before the parade of rafts started up again. The restrictions were to stay in effect while the Warden Service studied harlequin ducks in more detail.

The rafting community reacted with dismay and anger. May and June, while representing less than half the rafting season on the Maligne most years, provide cash flow during the period when larger rivers like the Athabasca are often in full flood. Although big rafts on the Athabasca account for most commercial rafting activity in Jasper, the Maligne is a unique, and therefore irreplaceable, recreational resource.

The relationship between the local rafting association and park management deteriorated rapidly; the commercial rafters hired a lawyer and launched a court challenge of the Superintendent's authority to restrict use of the river. They lost that case. After regrouping, they sued Parks Canada for civil damages resulting from cancellation of their business licences and the resulting financial losses. That case is still outstanding.

Park warden Bill Hunt was put in charge of coming up with the data to help solve both problems: declining ducks and angry rafters. He recognized a particularly frustrating irony in the situation.

"Those rafters," he pointed out, "are some of the most environmentally aware tourism operators in the park. When we asked them to voluntarily cut back their trips to three per day and to concentrate trips in the midday when the impact on ducks would be minimized, they complied. Maligne River Adventures even helped gather data on the ducks."

Nonetheless, he supported the interim closure. "Harlequin ducks return to the exact same breeding streams year after year. So if, in fact, those that remain on the Maligne gradually disappear without breeding successfully, it'll be a long time before we get any back. We have to play it safe in the short term, and try to get some broods off while we look for longer-term answers."

Harlequin ducks, Hunt points out, disappeared from Yoho National Park's heavily used Lake O'Hara area in the early 1980s and have never returned.

When more than half a million dollars annually is at stake, however, there is a lot of pressure for the kind of compromise that many had come to count on from Parks Canada. It would just be a small compromise, after all-but it would probably be illegal under the amended National Parks Act.

Besides, it is the cumulative impact of small compromises that has led to today's vast array of environmental problems and degraded ecosystems. If wintering habitat is subjected to oil spills, B.C. breeding streams are being shorn of cover and polluted by erosion from clearcuts, and recreational development is displacing harlequin ducks from still more streams, it may be that Canada's national parks aren't the place for further compromises but, instead, for leadership and hard decisions.

Dr. Geoff Holroyd has worked on endangered species conservation with the Canadian Wildlife Service for two decades. He is painfully aware of how much money and effort has to be invested for marginal returns when society tries to restore endangered species like the whooping crane or swift fox. "It is far more economical, and responsible," he says, "to keep species and populations from becoming endangered in the first place."

Biologists like Dr. Holroyd are used to stating such obvious truths only to be ignored. It must have been gratifying to him, then, when Parks Canada issued a new management plan for Jasper National Park in 2000. The revised plan permanently closed the middle Maligne River to all on-stream recreational use during the critical spring and early summer seasons. To mitigate the impact of that decision on commercial rafting companies, Parks Canada made portions of other rivers like the Whirlpool and Athabasca available for rafts. In justifying their decision, park authorities pointed to Bill Hunt's research findings as well as to the recommendations of an expert panel on the state of ecological integrity in Canada's national parks.

If the western harlequin duck joins its eastern relatives on the endangered list, it won't be because of uncontrolled human use in Jasper National Park. Nonetheless, securing the future of the Maligne's harlequin ducks carries a price tag. Business operators, who invested in expansion at a time when Parks Canada was finally beginning to come to terms with the cumulative costs of too much compromise, have paid an unfortunately large part of that price already.

The biggest price, however, has been in damaged relationships among the human players in the drama. From the harlequin ducks' point of view, the short-lived history of recreational rafting on Jasper's Maligne River had a happy ending. But no conservation success bought at the expense of community can really be considered a lasting victory, because by design it sows the seeds of future discord. Now that the middle Maligne River's ecosystem has begun to heal from too much human attention, other healing work—no less important—remains to be done.

Conservationists

Toad's Legacy

"*On the river, when you are finally on the river and you
are alone with a friend,
you can finally
let it go, all the rancour and the displacement
it does not matter here. They say I am a newcomer
and I say to them
get down to the river and say that, watch
the ducks fly up in laughter. This friend
knows the songs of all the birds by heart,
they are part of his heart
they are the reason he has a fighter's heart, he
stands up in the boat to see above the levees
and through the great black trees that
stand guard along the bank. We speak of
trees and mink and let it go.*

*"It goes by
and we drift through the world again like children,
after the first hour
we have settled in. An eagle hangs above us
like a man crucified to the sky.
There is a dead thing ahead, an elk
that crashed through the ice and turned instantly
to food for the ling, the suckered fish
following the canoe like shadows.
There is wind
there is the surface of the water rippled and stretched
by the wind. There is rot and the
smell of rot and there is finally a
blankness in the mind, it lets the eyes see again,
and the eyes look out from the dark heart itself*

and they let in the timeless light of the wild.

"They see the banks of the river,
carved and broken and sometimes dropping down
like mud, pale faceless mud. They see
line of sand upon line of gravel and we wonder out loud
how long it took,
we want to know about
the writing between the lines. But we do not expect
an answer, that is not why we are here today.
We want to feel
small because then we will also feel
as large as the eagle and the white world of swans..."

Excerpted from Dale (David) Zieroth's much longer poem "Columbia." Originally published in Mid-River, House of Anansi, 1976. Reprinted with permission.

On the river, as you drift around the first bend and the launch site vanishes behind cottonwoods, there is no point in worrying about time or things left undone. This is a different dimension now; the river will not be hurried. The brown water seems not so much to carry the canoe along as to hold it back, obliging paddlers to surrender to the timeless peace of the Columbia River wetlands.

Beyond the levees, screened from sight by tangles of alder, red-osier dogwood, willow and black cottonwood, the worried clamour of Canada geese and clucking of spotted frogs advertize unseen marshes and sloughs. Tracks of elk and deer pockmark muddy nicks in the river levees; sometimes bear or otter tracks appear too. Warbling vireos and ruby-crowned kinglets sing. Brown water hisses quietly in the branches of sweepers. Time slows nearly to a standstill.

My first float trip into the upper Columbia River's riparian wilderness was in 1975. Recently graduated, I had come to the edge of the Columbia Valley to work as a summer park naturalist. The green mosaic seemed to sprawl on forever, framed by mountains, humid, fecund, chaotic with birdsong. Ospreys, beavers, startled wood ducks and watchful herons: for a biology graduate trying to imagine his future the long float among new friends was a heady experience.

At the centre of it all was my boss for the summer: a stocky man with a brush cut, jean jacket and an impish grin. Ian Jack wore the air of unassuming competence that came naturally to foresters of his generation. He told us about a writer named Aldo Leopold, recounted humorous stories about old-time outfitters and modern-day hippies, and quietly made room for each of us in the circle of warmth around him. There seemed nothing he didn't know about birds, amphibians, bears and local history. In the evenings while we camped on old steamboat landings, his stories held us captive. As robins sang in the cottonwoods and cicadas trilled amid shadowed alders, Ian's distinctive chuckle punctuated the quiet buzz of conversation again and again.

"Ian used to like to watch people's behaviour on the Toad Floats," says Larry Halverson, a noted naturalist and environmental educator who lives at the southernmost edge of the wetlands in Invermere, B.C. He smiles at the memory of his close friend. "He always got a kick out of how some would start in paddling like they really had to get somewhere. Usually by the third day they'd have slowed down and be just drifting. Ian'd say to me, 'Looks like they finally found the toad.'"

The toad in question was a mythical beast Ian invented in the early 1970s. Spawned in the silty outwash of the Toby Glacier high in the Purcell Mountains west of Invermere, the great green toad was reputed to have migrated downstream to the marshes and backwaters of the upper Columbia River. The Columbia wetlands—sprawling across the bottom of the Rocky Mountain Trench from Athalmer 160 kilometres north, to the town of Donald—are the longest undisturbed riparian mosaic in North America today. The toad might be anywhere in there. Those who found him, Ian insisted, were certain to obtain wisdom and great blessings.

Beginning in 1973, Ian Jack and Larry Halverson organized annual expeditions to search for the great green Columbia River toad. Naturalists travelled from all over western Canada to join local conservationists for a three-day float down the river. In the middle of their motley flotilla, blinking like a mirror in the bright May sun, floated Ian Jack's aluminum rowboat. Over the years, Ian became known to his friends and admirers as Toad, and Toad Floats became less a quest for a mythical amphibian than a much-coveted opportunity to spend time with a man whose wisdom, humour and persistence will stand always as a model for those who want to make conservation work.

The river's sleepy rhythms may seem to slow time, but they cannot stop it. On November 9, 1996, Ian Jack collapsed and died of a heart attack while chopping wood at his home at Edgewater, just a few hundred metres from the wetlands he loved. He was only 60 years old. Unlike other great conservationists who died too young, however, Ian lived to see success after spending half his lifetime fighting for the Columbia wetlands. On April 30, 1996, barely six months before his death, the B.C. government signed an order establishing the new Columbia Wetlands Wildlife Management Area.

Larry Halverson, who took over from Ian as Chief Park Naturalist in Kootenay National Park after Ian's retirement, says that if there was any doubt about Ian's remarkable ability to unite diverse people around a common cause, his memorial service should have erased those. "Helicopter jockeys, loggers, hippies, trappers, hunters, politicians, coal miners—people of every kind were there." An overflow crowd of more than 250 people turned out to pay their last respects to the man who saved the Columbia River wetlands.

The odds seemed hopeless when Ian Jack first began the battle to save the wetlands. In the early 1970s, BC Hydro was determined to put those wetlands to work generating electric power. Prevailing public sentiment was that what was good for Hydro was good for B.C. The few who felt differently believed there was little point trying to stop the energy giant from implementing the Columbia River Treaty.

The Columbia River Treaty, signed in 1961 between Canada and the U.S.A., set the stage for a series of dams that destroyed nearly 600 kilometres of Canada's portion of the Columbia River. The Mica Dam, finished in 1973, backed the Columbia up into the Rocky Mountain Trench-a rift valley more than 1,000 kilometres long. The reservoir flooded hundreds of square kilometres of the valley floor, adding to damage already caused by the massive WAC Bennett Dam that, farther north, had plugged the Peace River in 1968 and backed water up both the Finlay and Parsnip River valleys to flood more than 1,600 square kilometres at the north end of the Rocky Mountain Trench. At the south end of the Trench the U.S. Army Corps of Engineers erected the Libby Dam on the Kootenay River, backing water into B.C. under Koocanusa Reservoir.

With most of the Rocky Mountain Trench already flooded, there was no practical way to dam the headwaters reach of the Columbia River upstream from the Mica Reservoir. But the treaty threatened it anyway.

Most of the Columbia River Treaty's hydropower and irrigation benefits went to the United States; the big reservoirs that flooded four-fifths of Canada's portion of the Columbia Valley merely stored water for American hydroelectric dams farther downstream. There was, however, one way that Canada could improve its returns: the treaty allowed BC Hydro to tip most of the Kootenay River's flow north into the Columbia at Canal Flats. There, instead of flowing south to turn turbines on the Libby Dam, it would flow through Canadian hydroelectric generating plants at the Mica and Revelstoke dams.

Ian Jack knew the upper Columbia River well. He hunted ducks, geese and deer among its lush backwater marshes and riparian thickets of willow and cottonwood. He volunteered his time to build nesting plat-forms for waterfowl and erect nest boxes for wood ducks and gold-eneyes. In spring, when willow catkins were yellow, song sparrows and redwings shouted about the return of another breeding season, and win-ter-weary deer congregated on newly green sidehills, Ian often floated down one of the Columbia's many twisting channels with Larry, Dale Zieroth or some other friend, soaking up sunshine, counting migrants and chuckling over his latest good story.

Most of his neighbours either didn't know about the proposed Kootenay-Columbia Diversion, or considered it pointless to resist BC

Hydro. Ian Jack, however, considered it a simple matter of values. It would be ethically wrong, he believed, to fail to protect the wetlands from a man-made flood. And so in the early 1970s he began a campaign that culminated more than a quarter century later in establishment of the Columbia River Wildlife Management Area.

Ian's strategy evolved as his network of contacts in the Columbia Basin grew. The Toad Floats helped introduce park naturalists and representatives of the outdoors media to the place itself, building awareness of the ecological values at stake and commitment to the cause of protection. Ian's sincere interest in and respect for people played no less important a role, because it yielded an ever-widening coalition of concern among town councils, local fish and game clubs, environmentalist groups and local businesses. Nobody, in Ian Jack's world, was an outsider. Everybody, in his view, was an environmentalist. His knack was in helping them realize it.

The diversion was a simple engineering issue to BC Hydro's planners. Ian's understanding of biology and the intimate workings of the wetland ecosystem, however, helped him frame the issue in terms engineers weren't comfortable working with.

"Ian just kept on asking them hard questions," says Larry Halverson, "and forcing them to go back and find answers rather than admit they hadn't really thought about what the effects might be. For example, the Kootenay River is a lot colder than the Columbia, so Ian asked how pouring all that colder water into the Columbia River would affect warmer-water fish like the pike-minnow, and the swimming and water-skiing on Lake Windermere."

Ian's questions echoed through the Columbia Valley, waking people to the many ways the diversion would undermine their well-being. Questions about cold water, for example, got the attention of Invermere's Chamber of Commerce. No less canny was Ian's question about what would happen—with most of the Kootenay River's flow diverted north—to the pollution from a large pulp mill on the Kootenay River at Skookumchuck. In the 1970s, dilution was still considered the solution to pollution; but with less dilution the pulp mill might be forced into costly technology upgrades. Ian's simple question produced another influential diversion opponent.

As his coalition continued to grow, their questions became more sophisticated and insistent and the costs, both in dollars and public goodwill, continued to mount. BC Hydro began to change its tune. By the 1980s water development projects no longer enjoyed the support they had two decades earlier. Energy conservation technology was emerging as a new way for electric utilities to make money. After waffling for several years, BC Hydro announced in 1990 that there would be no Kootenay-Columbia Diversion.

But the battle was far from over. Ironically, the diversion threat had actually protected the wetlands from other dangers. As long as BC Hydro held a flood reserve on the valley bottom, nobody seriously considered draining marshes for cropland, filling sloughs to create golf courses or developing recreational real estate. Now, with the threat of flooding gone, speculators began to look at the wildlife-rich wetlands and consider how to squeeze profits out of them.

The 1988 election of Mike Harcourt's NDP government, fortunately, had come just in time. The new government, hoping to put an end to divisive land use battles, announced a new planning initiative for every square centimetre of B.C.'s public land. Ian Jack retired from Parks Canada in 1992 and devoted himself full-time to representing the interests of hunters, anglers and other conservationists when the Commission on Resources and Environment (CORE) turned its attention to the East Kootenay region.

Bob Jamieson, a biologist-rancher from Ta Ta Creek who coordinated the East Kootenay CORE process, says that Ian was in his element in the CORE process. "Ian was one of those rare people who crossed over the line between naturalist and hunter," he says. "He could go out and shoot ducks in the morning, then spend the afternoon finding some rubber boas and making notes on them. He was the antithesis of the modern computer biologist. He learned from talking to the people, and he could talk with anyone." Ian's sheer enjoyment of people and consistent ability to steer conversations into the realm of shared values served him well in a process that demanded long hours of negotiation among people representing a diversity of conflicting interests—from logging and mining companies, government agencies, tourism operators and chambers of commerce to off-road vehicle groups, environmentalists and hunting outfitters.

"Ian and I both worked hard to get the wetlands protected," says Ellen Zimmerman, an eco-tourism operator from Golden, B.C. She represented the East Kootenay Environmental Society during the CORE negotiations. "But we wanted a Class A Provincial Park and Ian wanted a Wildlife Management Area."

Under B.C. protected areas legislation, a Wildlife Management Area protects habitat from development while still providing for recreational uses such as hunting, fishing, nature study and eco-tourism where they don't conflict with wildlife needs. Ian preferred to keep the wetlands exactly as they were and not risk disenfranchising any of the traditional users who had, after all, played so important a role in the earlier battle against the diversion. He suspected a provincial park might result in new recreational development, more tourism and less room for traditional users.

Ultimately, Ian's vision won the day and, as usual, his wisdom proved itself when a controversy over motorized vehicles erupted only six months after his death. Participants in the 1997 Toad Float, which Larry Halverson organized in memory of Ian and in honour of his widow, Joyce, encountered several aggressive stunters on motorized jetskis. The experience spurred several participants to start looking into the impacts of motorized boats and other vehicles on wildlife. A provincial park, with its recreational mandate, might not have supported their subsequent call for restrictions on motors. However, the Wildlife Management Area had to put wildlife needs first. The B.C. government quickly imposed a year-round 10-horsepower restriction on motorized traffic in the wetlands.

"The order includes all motorized conveyances, including snowmobiles, quads, dirt bikes, jet boats and so on," says Dave Phelps, Regional Land Management Biologist responsible for the wetlands. "It was implemented to reduce disturbance and harassment of wintering wildlife; soil erosion and sedimentation on forage plants and invertebrates; harassment; predation on waterfowl broods that scatter after being surprised by high-speed craft; egg breakage from rapid flight off nests; and general habitat destruction."

It also restored the stillness.

One recent May evening, I picked my way down a narrow forest trail to Larry Halverson's rustic cabin on the edge of the Columbia River near Brisco. A kestrel harassed a bald eagle above the cottonwoods as I unloaded my gear and strolled down to the water's edge. A few hundred metres away, a massive stick nest dwarfed the poplar that held it. A white head showed above the rim; the eagle's mate was incubating eggs. A pike-minnow splashed in a nearby eddy.

It had been years since I had been down to the Columbia wetlands, but as I lowered myself into the grass and looked across the marshes at mountains hazed by the smoke of distant fires, I felt the old familiar quiet seeping into me. In a world with too much change, this was a place where almost nothing had changed. Geese still clamoured beyond the alders. Warbling vireos and ruby-crowned kinglets sang just as they had every other May morning for centuries. The green world enfolded me, welcoming me back.

Last time I was here, I had visited with Ian. He was putting up goose nesting platforms. It occurred to me now that Ian had been here on all my previous visits to this place. Suddenly conscious of a deep sense of loss, I listened for the rattle of an oar against the side of an aluminum rowboat or the sound of mirthful laughter. All I heard, however, was birdsong and the timeless whisper of passing water; and after a while I realized that was enough.

The Toad was there. And he always will be.

Hope on the Range

Another April chinook is spilling down across the Alberta foothills. Prairie crocuses dance in the wind as they've done here every spring for centuries.

The wind sweeping out of Waterton Lakes National Park chases rippling waves through brown fescue. Trumpeter swans and Canada geese dot the quiet wetland below the crocus-covered ridge. A grizzly bear roots about beneath the nearby aspens, unearthing sweet glacier lily bulbs and pocket gophers. Two sandhill cranes strut and croak. The thin sweetness of a horned lark's song tinkles in the wind.

The grizzly emerges from the aspens and pauses to rub his heavy muzzle in the tangled bunchgrass. Unaware of him until now, several cows on the nearby ridge begin to bawl for their recently born calves. The bear watches with lazy interest as mothers gather calves and the herd crashes away into silver willow shrubbery along the base of the far hillside. Then he shakes himself and moseys down to the water's edge, investigating the odours to be found there.

Undisturbed by scent or sight of humans, he has spent all week here, in some of the most productive habitat occupied by grizzlies anywhere in Canada-a mosaic of rich wetlands, aspen forest and bunchgrass prairie. He cleaned up the remains of two stillborn calves earlier this month but it's mostly the greenery that interests him today.

The same combination of productive natural habitat and lack of human activity that makes this foothills haven good for bears benefits the cranes and swans too. Both will produce broods of offspring here later this spring. Amid the cow tracks down by the slough are the tracks of elk and deer. They, too, thrive in the solitude of the aspen parkland that stretches along the foot of the Rocky Mountains here beneath the chinook arch.

For those who visit nearby Waterton Lakes National Park, this diversity of wildlife and habitat might seem unremarkable. The spectacular, but compact, park-designated an International Biosphere Reserve in 1977 and a World Heritage Site in 1995-is famous for its abundant wildlife.

The grizzly, cranes and trumpeter swans, however, are on privately owned ranchland several kilometres northeast of the park. Much of Waterton's wildlife wealth is, in fact, less a product of park protection than of habitat ranchers outside the park have protected for more than a century. Almost all the region's sandhill cranes and trumpeter swans nest on private ranchland. Some rare plants like blue camas and blue flag iris are virtually unknown inside the park, but are abundant on neighbouring cattle pastures. Even grizzly bears, although their opportunistic feeding habits sometimes bring them into conflict with ranchers, are often more abundant on foothills ranches outside the park boundaries than inside the park.

Waterton is a paradox that confounds those who look for simple solutions to conservation challenges. Its wildlife abundance is at least as much the result of cattle ranching as it is of park protection. To many naturalists, the whole idea seems counterintuitive: aren't cows bad? Don't ranchers kill predators? How can a park not only coexist with, but also depend on, cattle ranching?

"Make no mistake about it," says the Nature Conservancy of Canada's western field director Larry Simpson. "If the ranches vanish from the Waterton Front, there is no future for Waterton Lakes National Park."

Dave Glaister agrees, as might be expected of a man who's raised cattle for well more than half a century. But the tall, lean rancher-naturalist is less concerned with proving that ranches help conserve biological diversity than simply ensuring that ranching will survive in a changing world. He isn't sure it can. Like the solitude-loving wildlife that lives on his family's Shoderee Ranch, north of Waterton, he's retreated before the tidal wave of development about as far as he can go. Glaister and many other ranchers are starting to know how it feels to be an endangered species.

Dave and Lucille Glaister raised their family west of Millarville, Alberta. Their ranch sprawled along the edge of the Bow-Crow Forest Reserve, in a foothills landscape rich in deer, elk, bear and moose. It was prime cattle-growing country, and a fine place to raise kids-perfect in all respects except one. It was only a half hour's drive from Calgary.

They don't live there any more. Their former ranch is now subdivided into small acreages, most of which house "rurban" commuters who work in the booming city, then retreat each night to half million dollar homes in the scenic foothills. Each acreage has its own roadway, lawn and buildings. Many feed horses on undersized, overgrazed pastures. Pet cats hunt in the underbrush and family dogs chase deer at night. Yard lights have banished the undisturbed darkness that used to greet the Glaisters when they rose before dawn.

Until recently, the Alberta foothills were among the last places where Canada's prairie ecosystem seemed likely to survive. Elsewhere, most has been lost to cultivation and urban development. The earliest, and greatest, losses were in western Ontario and Manitoba where much less than one percent of the tallgrass prairie survives uncultivated. The fescue grassland region, extending from western Manitoba in a fertile arch through Saskatoon and Edmonton south to Calgary, fared little better. The somewhat drier mixedgrass region is Canada's wheat belt: miles and miles of rolling grain stubble stitched together with barbed wire fences. Ghost bison graze among granaries and grid roads.

Only those parts of the prairie too dry for cultivation or with too short a growing season survived the 20th century's epidemic of landscape change-and those are where ranchers now face the next wave of land conversion.

Ranching country is scenic, wildlife-rich and relatively inexpensive for those seeking a recreational hideaway or a scenic setting for a commuter home. Instead of cultivating the grassland, subdivisions and acreages carve it into weedy little bits. Grizzlies aren't welcome in acreage country: some residents might appreciate them but their neighbours don't. Wolves are a romantic idea until they run the family horse through the fence. Upland sandpipers, long-billed curlews and sharp-tailed grouse can't adapt to patchwork prairie patrolled by pet dogs and cats.

The Glaisters sold their ranch when the trickle of new acreages around them became a flood. They liked some of the new neighbours, but trespassers, stray pets and other petty problems continued to increase. As land prices inflated, they could no longer afford to lease pasture or buy new land. Their taxes grew past the point where the economically marginal business of growing cattle could yield a reasonable income.

Larry Simpson puts the financial dilemma faced by development-besieged ranchers in perspective. "Land in the Alberta foothills was worth about $100 per acre in 1971," he says. "Today land sells for 10 to 18 times more. But cattle prices-well, back then you would have to sell maybe 10 calves to buy a truck. Today it takes between 40 and 50. So beef prices have comparatively gone down while land prices have gone up."

Dave and Lucille, and their grown children, decided to get as far away from Calgary's fevered real estate market as possible when they sold the family ranch in 1991. Their search for a more remote refuge led them to the Shoderee, one of prairie Canada's last large ranches. The Shoderee sprawls along Pine Ridge, a long moraine carpeted with rough fescue grassland and aspen forest that connects westward with Waterton Lakes National Park's windy mountains.

At night, on the Shoderee, no lights show in any direction. By day, red-tailed hawks scream above the aspens, the sounds of geese and cranes carry from hidden sloughs, and the woods and willow tangles are a bedlam of birdsong. The family regularly see grizzly bears. From time to time they see wolves too.

"One morning I was having breakfast," says Glaister, who keeps a spotting scope mounted in the living room for watching wildlife, "and I saw 15 whitetail bucks go out across the hay field. One after another, 15 of them."

The Glaisters love the wildness and diversity of their new home. They barely had time to settle in, however, before the juggernaut they had fled was at the door.

Quarter sections—normally the smallest un-subdivided unit of ranchland—adjacent to the Shoderee have recently sold for $1200/acre. Smaller acreages have sold for $40,000/acre. No rancher can hope to pay the carrying costs on that kind of money simply by raising cattle. As land prices increase, in fact, even established ranchers who own their land outright find themselves caught in a tax squeeze; recently the Alberta government passed new legislation that forces municipalities to tax land based on its current market value. Some landowners have seen their yearly tax bills triple or quadruple simply because of their location adjacent to one of the hottest recreational destinations anywhere: the Canadian Rockies.

Area ranchers are no longer surprised to return home after a long day to find a real estate broker's card tucked into their screen door. "Even the ones I've run off already do it," says one local rancher. "They just wait until they see me go out."

Larry Simpson says that the Nature Conservancy of Canada has begun to focus on the ranching country along the eastern slopes of the Alberta Rockies "...because all the conservation values are there, including predators. Sure there are conflicts that occur from time to time but the fact remains that those animals are there because the habitat exists. Landscapes can recover from most everything but not from concrete."

Simpson represents an organization that calls itself the real estate arm of the conservation movement. His job is to invest donated money so as to get the greatest return in conservation of endangered nature. Spending other people's money is a big responsibility, so he does his homework. Real estate experts he has consulted predict that as many as 60 percent of the ranches in western North American will be sold in the first 20 years of the 21st century. An entire generation of ranchers is nearing retirement age; many have complicated estates to settle. If current real estate trends continue, many of their ranches will end up in the hands of speculators and developers.

Like Dave Glaister, Larry Simpson is tall and lean, but the resemblance stops there. Simpson has an intense, focused personality. He seems driven by urgency—like time is running out. Indeed, he says, it is: "The western heritage and natural heritage of western North America could potentially undergo a transformation in the next 20 years that will be as profound and long reaching as the loss of the bison. Different, yes: but no less significant."

Larry Simpson uses satellite images of Canada to make his case for what he calls Canada's one percent challenge. For all Canada's vast size, he points out, only one percent of the country is both arable and biologically intact. That one percent—mostly in the dry southern prairies or in a thin arc along the Alberta foothills—contains almost half of all Canada's endangered species. And that one percent continues to die the death of many cuts as gas pipelines slice through native prairie, towns and cities grow, and, with increasing regularity, ranchers give up the struggle and cash in by selling their land to developers.

In the late 1990s the Nature Conservancy of Canada launched what Simpson calls the Waterton Front Project: an ambitious campaign to permanently protect at least eight major ranches adjacent to Waterton. Already the Nature Conservancy has placed conservation easements on several square kilometres of land and has other deals pending. Larry Simpson points out, however, that the same pressures that beset Waterton are at play in the Crowsnest Pass, the Porcupine Hills and the foothills west of Calgary and Red Deer. The challenge is as immense as it is urgent.

"If Canada fails to meet our one percent challenge, with our level of education and relative affluence compared with other nations, that suggests to me that the world must almost surely fail in conserving biological diversity."

Others share Simpson's sense of urgency. World Wildlife Fund Canada released its Prairie Conservation Action Plan in 1989, stating: "In only 100 years, the Canadian prairies—grasslands and parkland—have been so radically transformed by human activity that they have become one of the most endangered natural regions in Canada...Canadians need to ensure that native prairie, with its wild plants and animals, survives in the west and is conserved for its intrinsic values, from which this and future generations can benefit."

All this is true, but why worry about ranching? Cattle, after all, are not bison. Cattle can overgraze prairie, helping weeds invade and reducing food and cover for native wildlife. Cows are notorious for spending too much time in riparian areas where they trample and graze wildlife habitat and damage streambanks. Ranchers have rarely been noted for generous feelings toward large predators. It was agricultural "pest" control, in fact, that erased grizzly bears and wolves from much of their North American range.

American conservation writer George Wuerthner goes so far as to argue that subdivisions are better than ranching. In the American west, private land is more limited in extent than in southern Canada. Once ranching is no longer viable there, he says, nearby public lands can start to recover from decades of cattle damage. His argument, however, has a fundamental flaw since the private lands are usually the most ecologically productive habitats: those along valley floors and streams that early homesteaders scooped up first.

Most of the range damage American conservationists complain about dates back to the late 1800s when eastern speculators poured millions of cattle into the open range. Especially in the arid and semi-arid grasslands west of the Rockies, where native vegetation evolved in the absence of large herds of grazing animals, the damage was massive.

Canada, according to historian Barry Potyondi, never suffered the massive overstocking of open range that took place farther south. Overgrazing was only a local problem that appeared in the 20th century as growing numbers of hopeful colonists fenced and cross-fenced the range, confining cattle into smaller and smaller tracts of grassland and reducing the economic margins within which ranchers had to operate.

Most of Canada's rangeland lies east of the Rockies where vegetation evolved under the influence of large herds of bison. Spared frontier overgrazing, Canada's grasslands actually benefit from cattle ranching, which promotes vegetation diversity. The key is well-managed grazing—management that approximates what the native grassland was used to before the arrival of the domestic cow. After a century of ranching, most ranchers who are still in business have proven their ability to keep native ranges healthy.

Riparian damage is a different problem; many ranches still have so-called "sacrifice areas" down by the creek where cows spend too much time. In the past decade, however, a growing riparian restoration movement has spread across Alberta, southern B.C. and Saskatchewan. Rather than giving their herds year-round access to creek bottoms, ranchers fence out riparian pastures and develop wells or dugouts to provide water to their herds when they are on upland areas. By grazing riparian areas only when soils and vegetation are most resistant to damage, participating ranchers restore the willow thickets, reedgrass swales and cottonwood forests that make prairie riparian areas some of the most productive and important habitats in prairie Canada.

Predators remain a thorny issue. The Glaisters have lost cattle to grizzlies. Nearby ranchers have lost stock to wolves. Those who view foothills grasslands primarily as cattle country rarely harbour warm feelings toward animals that can kill livestock. Even so, ranchers like the Glaisters value the presence of large predators, only calling in problem wildlife officers when they actually suffer livestock losses. The irony, of course, is that wolves and grizzly bears still range many parts of the Alberta foothills only because ranching, which keeps the landscape largely natural, ensures that they can find wild prey and, in the case of the bears, a diversity of plant foods. In southwestern Alberta, recently, some ranchers have begun working cooperatively with Alberta Environmental Protection to head off predator-livestock conflicts before they happen.

Most of the environmental criticisms aimed at ranching relate to management practices that can be, and increasingly are being, remedied. Meantime, as long as ranching families like the Glaisters can keep the land intact and make a reasonable living at ranching, the last and best that remains of prairie Canada's biological diversity will have a fighting chance.

"A well-managed ranch operation," says Larry Simpson, "is a living, working model of a steady state economy. If the entire world could be managed and kept in as good condition as many ranches, then we would be in good environmental shape."

His Royal Highness Prince Phillip, the Duke of Edinburgh, was in

Regina for the launch of the Prairie Conservation Plan. "There are those who know and understand the serious consequences for the future health of this planet if ecosystems are wantonly destroyed," he said, "and there are those who have the power or the influence or the resources to prevent that destruction...The solution is to establish two-way communication between these groups."

As well-heeled urbanites and developers drive up the real estate value of Canada's best surviving grassland ecosystems, ranchers like the Glaisters are losing their power to continue protecting the places they love. Larry Simpson is determined to ensure that they don't stand alone.

Man for the Mountains

The rain has ended. Clouds are shredding themselves against the peaks up the Waterton Valley. Golden sun streams through a gap in the west and fills the valley below with emerald green, as if the land were lit from within. A lazuli bunting in a nearby aspen sings as if mesmerized by the surreal stillness of this June evening. The air smells of wild roses and new green foliage.

For a while conversation stops and the people gathered on the porch at Hawk's Nest find themselves lost together in the utter calm and glowing beauty of the moment. There are a dozen of us here this evening, conservationists gathered from across the country to plan how to protect this landscape from the forces of fragmentation that have already destroyed so much of Canada's wilderness beauty. Some are wealthy philanthropists determined to invest in nature's future. Others represent conservation organizations like the Nature Conservancy of Canada. A couple of us are biologists. Sitting in an old armchair at the corner of the porch, a big man with a black cowboy hat and fringed coat catches my eye and grins. He's watched this view thousands of times before. He knows that when the sun dips behind Horseshoe Ridge and the humid evening chill comes spilling out of the shadows beneath the aspens, the spell will break and the group will move indoors. In the warmth of the old hunting lodge, as owls begin to hoot outside, it will be time for another kind of magic.

For now, let the beauty of southern Alberta's grizzly country speak to the spirits of those gathered here to help protect it. Later, Andy Russell will speak to their imaginations as he has already done so many times before. That is, after all, why they are here.

There isn't a lot about Andy Russell—at least not on first appearance—to suggest that this man has become a living icon of Canada's conservation movement. His hair is silver-grey, his face tanned and chiselled with lines from wind and age, and he doesn't stand as straight as he used to. He's an old-timer now, with the slow drawl and ready laugh of a cowboy.

But let him ease back and fix you with his hawk-like eyes, let him fish around in his mind for the right story for the occasion and it won't take long to discover that the old man of the mountains has lost none of the wisdom, acerbity, humour and power that have made him a force to be reckoned with for more than 50 years.

Perhaps more than any 20th-century Canadian conservationist, Andy Russell helped define both our wilderness movement, and our collective understanding and concern for wild animals and wild places. His uncanny talent for storytelling transformed the lives and minds of an entire generation by awakening them to the meaning of wilderness and challenging their complacency about its well-being. And his bull-headed passion for fairness and refusal to be intimidated won lasting changes in how governments and industry respect their obligations to the environment.

If there is hope for reconciliation between people and the places where we live in the 21st century, it will be in no small part due to Andy Russell's contribution to the century just past.

As surely as the sun rises tomorrow morning, grizzly country is wilderness country, and he cannot live without it. Man, through most of his recent evolution from primitive to present-day civilization, has chosen to fight the wilderness blindly, attempting to break nature to his needs, at war with it and sometimes mercilessly destroying the very things he needs the most. The grizzly can show us something of what it means to live in harmony with nature. Grizzly Country, 1967

I was in Grade 10 the year my sister gave my father a copy of Andy Russell's newly released Grizzly Country for Christmas. It sat on the coffee table in our Calgary home for weeks before I picked it up one day and idly flipped through it, looking at photos of grizzly bears, bighorn sheep and wild places.

Once I started reading the text, I was captured. During the following week, I read Andy Russell's book from cover to cover, twice. It was like nothing I had ever read before, a deeply lived and deeply thought chronicle of adventure and discovery in the wild country of western North America. Woven through the personal anecdotes and vivid story-telling were well-researched facts about an animal that, at that time, was more a figure of fearful imagination than a real creature to most North Americans.

Until then, to a boy growing up in Calgary, the Rocky Mountains had been little more than a blue-grey wall along the western horizon. Some days, especially when a chinook arch spilled across the sky, they seemed magnified, close, crisp with detail. Other days they receded into distance, becoming vaguely unreal.

Grizzly Country—and after it, *Horns in the High Country*—had the effect of turning my face toward those mountains more than ever before. It had never occurred to me that wildness might be so close to home. Hiking the hills on the outskirts of Calgary alone, or fishing with Dad and my siblings along some quiet foothills stream, I would look west to where steep-sided valleys receded into shadows among the peaks and hear Andy Russell's stories whispering to me of what might lie just beyond. An entirely new world of wilderness had opened up for me.

What I didn't know at the time was that I was not alone in feeling the powerful effect of Andy's words. Before the late 1960s, few Canadians had concerned themselves about wildlife and the environment. My generation was born into one of the longest economic boom periods in the country's history. The 1950s and 1960s were an era of brash confidence and rapid development. It seemed like our natural resources could never run out.

Andy Russell's books played a crucial role in awakening Canadians' awareness to the costs of too much mindless progress. While his seemingly endless wealth of personal anecdotes awakened a fascination and longing in the hearts of many readers, he was blunt about pointing out the rate of landscape destruction and its consequences to the Rockies. His writings were distillations of nostalgia for frontier times and people, love of wild nature and urgent concern about the rate of change and loss.

Reading his books, I realized that Andy Russell was in many ways like my father. Like Dad, he'd lived through most of the changes that characterized the 20th century. He shared my father's love for fishing, hiking and hunting. So there was a kind of symmetrical rightness to the fact that my first chance to meet Andy Russell in the flesh was in 1974 when the University of Calgary honoured both him and my Dad with honorary doctorates: Dad for a lifetime of service to education, and Andy for his lifetime of service to conservation.

That was 26 years ago. Since then, Andy has added another lifetime of service to conservation, and he now holds four honorary doctorates.

Andy Russell's life began as the frontier came to an end. He was born in the southern Alberta town of Lethbridge in 1915, and spent his earliest years on a ranch beside the St. Mary River. He grew up surrounded by people who had lived the beginning of the western frontier: wolfers, trappers, Blood and Stoney Indians, ranch hands and teamsters. When he was still a young boy, his family moved west into the foothills of the Rockies, settling near the headwaters of Drywood Creek.

Radios were rare and television undreamed of in those days. Many rural homes didn't even have electricity. Evenings were long and quiet. In the quiet glow of oil lamps, or outside around flickering campfires, conversation was the chief form of entertainment. Andy recalls sneaking into the edge of the campfire glow as a small boy and listening, spellbound, to the stories of old frontiersmen.

After dropping out of high school, Andy worked as a trapper and hunting guide in the wild and windy country along the eastern edges of the Rocky Mountains. In 1936, at the age of 19, he left home and signed on as a packer and guide for a famous Waterton-area outfitter named Bert Riggall. He refined his storytelling art around countless campfires.

During his years with Riggall, Andy Russell travelled thousands of kilometres by packtrain through the upper Oldman drainage, B.C.'s Flathead watershed and the spectacular wildlands of the upper Castle and Waterton rivers. Alberta's oil and gas industry had not yet awakened to the possibility of petroleum beneath the mountains, so few mountain valleys had yet been marred by roads. Thousands of bighorn sheep roamed the windy ridges, grizzly bears foraged along floodplains and avalanche slopes, and growing numbers of elk ranged the open timber. The youthful Andy had all this and Bert Riggall too—an English-born botanist and photographer with a naturalist's gift for observation and interpretation. It was wealth beyond all imagining, and fertile soil for the conservation activist and nature writer that still lay latent in this gangling young ranch kid with a knack for handling horses and telling stories.

Andy's boss also had two daughters. Kay, the eldest, often travelled with the packtrains, cooking and managing the camps. In 1938 Andy and Kay married, spending their honeymoon where they had spent their courtship—exploring wild country on horseback. When Bert retired in 1946, Andy and Kay took over the outfitting business. They eventually moved into a small bungalow on their ranch just north of Waterton.

But things were changing in the backcountry. During the post-war boom years of the 1950s, the Alberta government discovered that oil development made for happy voters and flush treasuries. There was little political gain in regulating petroleum firms, so government instead put its energy into promoting development. While government engineers built new gravel roads up major river valleys, oil company bulldozers fanned out across the landscape, slicing new seismic lines into once-pristine wilderness.

For Andy and Kay Russell, the new roads spelled the end of a golden era. Well-heeled clients weren't willing to pay to be packed into country others could drive to. "I knew that outfitting was finished, at least the way I'd known it," says Andy. "We were among the top three outfits in North America at that time but it didn't matter. I'd seen some of these other guys try to hang on and it was just pitiable to see what happened."

Andy stopped outfitting in 1960. He retained his pack stock and outfit, however, and put them to work for an ambitious new undertaking. After years of close observation of grizzlies, bighorns and other wildlife in their wilderness homes, Andy decided to try his hand at creating nature movies. If he could no longer take urban people into the dwindling wilderness, perhaps he could take wilderness to them in the cities and try to awaken popular concern over the loss of wildlife and wild places. He knew grizzlies and other wilderness animals were becoming scarce, but he also knew that few others were aware, or cared.

His first two efforts were doomed by lack of familiarity with the business side of film-making. In 1961, he and his oldest sons, Dick and Charlie, headed into the high country to film a third movie, this one on grizzly bears. Working with heavy camera gear and dealing with the vagaries of weather, terrain and animal behaviour, the film crew took three years to complete the movie.

During 1962 and 1963, much of Andy's filming took place not in the Rockies, but in Alaska's Denali National Park. The crew could not carry firearms for protection. A lifetime of experience with grizzlies had already taught the Russells that the bears are far less dangerous than their reputation had suggested. But even Andy and his sons were surprised by how tolerant the bears were, as long as the crew paid attention to bear body language, backing off when a grizzly wanted to feed or wander through an area the crew was already occupying. Previously, with the unconscious arrogance that firearms give humans, they had not been nearly so sensitive to the signals bears gave them. It was an important lesson about the potential for peaceful coexistence between grizzlies and humans: all they needed to do was deal with the bears humbly and respectfully.

Andy needed money to pay for the cost of production of the movie, so he came up with the idea of writing a book. He'd already written a number of magazine articles, mostly for American hunting and fishing magazines.

"I flew down to New York," he says, "and had lunch with the editor-in-chief of Alfred A. Knopf Publishing. I had about a hundred pictures that I showed him over lunch, full-frame photos of mule deer and bighorns—I had one there of just the head and shoulders of a grizzly—and he asked me how the hell I got pictures like that. I told him that was what I was there for, and I wanted to write him a book. He sent me home with a $3,000 advance."

Grizzly Country sold tens of thousands of copies and was translated into more than a dozen languages. It is still in print, more than a quarter of a century after it first came out in 1967. Andy took the movie on the road soon after the release of his book. The book's runaway success guaranteed him sell-out audiences.

At first, however, Andy faced a torrent of criticism for portraying grizzlies as peace-loving animals and describing filming them without protection. "I was condemned for that book by some people. They said I was endangering people out on the trail because they'd believe what they read and get in trouble with bears. The Chief Naturalist in Jasper National Park gave me hell."

Whatever the popular prejudice might have been about grizzly bears at the time—Andy recalls the curator of the New York Zoological Society describing the retiring omnivores as among the three fiercest predators in North America—the movie footage Andy took on the road could not be denied. Clearly, this animal had received a bum rap from people whose prejudices and fears got in the way of their ability to observe and think.

Andy spent 11 years showing that movie. He took it all over North America and filled big theatres everywhere he went. Some nights it was standing room only. "But it was a tough way to make a dollar, living out of a suitcase and having to deal with different strangers all the time."

Other books followed on the heels of Grizzly Country: Trails of a Wilderness Wanderer (1971), Horns of the High Country (1973), The Rockies (1975) and Memoirs of a Mountain Man (1984). Between books Andy researched, wrote and taped more than 500 episodes for a popular radio series on Alberta's history sponsored by TransAlta Ltd. He also did speaking tours, television appearances and numerous magazine articles. One way or another, he made well and sure nobody missed hearing what he had to say.

Internationally, Andy Russell is known for his films and his books, but closer to home, he's also known for rolling up his sleeves and wading into the nearest dogfight when wildlife and the environment are threatened.

There was the coyote incident, for example. Back in the 1960s, predators had even fewer friends than they have now. Agricultural service boards considered poisoning coyotes to be just one part of a holy war to make southern Canada safe for chickens and sheep. In waging their war, some took shortcuts. A rancher neighbour of Andy's stopped him one day in Pincher Creek to tell him about the dead coyotes he'd been finding around his ranch in the south Porcupine Hills. Local agricultural field agents had been lacing the carcasses of dead horses with Compound 1080, a deadly nerve poison, and leaving them out on the range. It was a coyote-killing technique as effective as it was illegal. The rancher had complained about the illegal baits, which posed a danger not only to other wildlife but to ranch dogs and even children, but had not had any success. What, he asked, could they do to change the situation?

"I said, 'Howard, can you get us some of those coyotes?'" Andy recalls, a glint in his eye. It was May, sunny springtime in the Alberta foothills. Howard managed to retrieve 10 coyotes in various states of decomposition. "Well, about 10," Andy says. "Some were just pieces. They were pretty ripe."

The friends knew that the Agricultural Service Board had a meeting scheduled the next day in Pincher Creek. Andy placed a phone call to some of his television news contacts in Lethbridge and suggested they might get some good footage if they could get a camera crew to Pincher Creek by 10 that morning.

When the municipal councillors and agricultural staff arrived for their meeting, they found news cameras trained on them and several foul-smelling coyote carcasses spread out on the lawn. "Oh, man, those things stank," Andy laughs. "That air was so thick you could have cut it up and built a fence with it. They were just livid."

Overnight, says Andy, there ceased to be a problem with illegal coyote baits. And once again Andy had acquired some new friends, as well as new enemies.

Andy first stepped outside the calm currents of conformity and began to make waves—and adversaries—in the cause of conservation back in the mid-1940s. He says his moment of truth came over what now seems a relatively minor issue. In those days, a group of local ranchers had permits to graze several hundred head of cattle inside Waterton Lakes National Park. Elk commonly moved out of the park in winter to forage on the same ranchers' haystacks. The ranchers wanted something done about the elk, and they held a meeting in the park to discuss the problem. Andy was the secretary-treasurer of the grazing association.

"I was sitting there taking notes and listening about the elk bothering them," Andy recalls. "They weren't a bit concerned about the park grass. And I thought, 'Andy Russell, it is time for you to rare up.'" Andy asked the chairman for permission to speak. He then asserted that it seemed a bit ridiculous for his neighbouring ranchers to be so concerned about elk coming down on their haystacks when, in his view, their cattle were eating most of the winter elk feed in the summertime.

"Oh brother! They'd like to have shot me. One of those fellows never forgave me. To the day he died, he never forgave me."

Andy's first conservation adversaries may have been his fellow ranchers, but since then he has put far more energy into protecting ranchers' interests. His most frequent adversaries, not surprisingly, have been big oil and the Alberta government. In 1957 Shell Canada discovered one of Canada's richest sour gas deposits in the mountains of southwestern Alberta. The company promptly began construction of its giant Shell-Waterton sour gas processing plant beside Drywood Creek, almost within spitting distance of the ranch where Andy grew up. Some of the most heartbreakingly beautiful country in the world—Andy's old outfitting territory—was soon defiled by roads and pipelines. Toxic chemicals from the processing plant killed fish in Drywood Creek. Sulphur dust blew from stockpiles into surrounding pastures, acidifying the soil. Hydrogen sulphide gas and other contaminants spread downwind. Through the 1960s and 1970s Andy was at the forefront of repeated battles over industrial pollution and land abuse.

His running war against industrial greed came to a head in the early 1980s when Andy and Zahava Hannan, a rancher near Millarville, took on two of the largest oil companies in the world. Esso owned an aging gas processing plant near Hannan's ranch. Shell Canada had found a large deposit of highly poisonous sour gas in the foothills to the west.

The two companies applied jointly to the Alberta Energy Resources Conservation Board—the regulatory agency—for permission to run a high pressure pipeline from Shell's Moose Mountain field to Esso's Quirk Creek plant. The plant would remove the toxic sulphur before shipping the natural gas to market.

Zahava Hannan had already documented a long series of problems with industrial pollution near her ranch. Andy Russell suspected that the aging plant would not be able to handle the increased load. One explosion or leak of the deadly gas would have had devastating consequences.

But trying to stop the project would not be easy. The regulatory board received its funding in equal parts from oil companies and the government's energy department. Consequently, it had an established pattern of ruling in favour of industry, no matter how valid the concerns of local residents might be.

When the board convened a 10-day public hearing on the pipeline proposal, Andy and his partner intervened. In that first hearing, they faced intimidating cross-examination. "It was perfectly obvious what they were trying to do with us," says Andy. "Everybody was running from these guys and had been for years. Well, I wasn't and I wasn't going to start either."

A hearing that was supposed to last only 10 days ended up stretching on for three years-the longest hearing in the board's history. Phalanxes of well-paid lawyers and engineers faced off against the two ranchers. "They didn't know what to do with us," says Andy. "One time I was in the washroom at the Calgary courthouse at noon and I was in one of the booths. In comes Shell's lawyer and the lawyer that was working for the government. And the one guy says to the other, 'You know the trouble with Andy Russell is, he says the damnedest things and people believe him.' I had a heck of a time trying to keep quiet in that booth."

Though Andy and Zahava Hannan hired a former Shell engineer and an up-and-coming Calgary lawyer to fight their case for them, there's no doubt that Andy's public profile also played an important role in the battle. The two ranchers eventually won. Their David-and-Goliath struggle helped change the way in which government regulated Alberta's energy industry.

Shortly afterward, Andy Russell was on the warpath again—this time over a dam the Alberta government proposed to build on the Oldman River north of Pincher Creek. Again, he lent his name and personal credibility to a grassroots battle against overwhelming odds; in this case, the powerful alliance of government water engineers, irrigation lobbyists and private engineering companies that had already dammed most other southern Alberta rivers. Once again, power brokers were shocked out of complacency as the Friends of the Oldman River won battle after battle. In the end, however, the dam builders won by simply ignoring the rulings of regulatory boards and courts. Andy Russell's 1987 book The Life of a River remains a lasting indictment of the Alberta government's short-sighted obsession with resource development in the 20th century. Although the Oldman River was lost, the fight over it helped save Alberta's Milk and Quebec's Great Whale rivers from similar fates.

Andy Russell's wife Kay died in 1984. He has lived alone for more than 15 years now. He has slowed down a little and now gets as much enjoyment out of the achievements of his children and grandchildren as he once did from his own.

Two sons, Dick and John, have worked as wildlife biologists for decades. John, a caribou and bear biologist, lives just down the hill from Hawk's Nest. Charlie visits from time to time when he isn't at his cabin in Russia's remote Kamchatka Peninsula with artist Maureen Enns, testing their theories about peaceful coexistence between grizzly bears and humans. Two other Russell offspring, Gordon and Anne, live within a few hours of the family home. Charlie's son Anthony, Andy Russell's oldest grandchild, works as a Banff National Park warden. Conservation and love of wild nature run in the blood of all the Russell clan.

Even so, Andy Russell is not yet ready to sit back and leave others to do all the fighting for wild places and wild things. He continues to champion conservation causes even now, well into his ninth decade on this earth. Lately, he has turned his attention to heading off the threat real estate development poses to the wildlife, habitat and cultural traditions of the foothills ranching landscape that gave shape and meaning to his life. The oil and gas industry has not heard the last of him either—Andy has plans to organize an investigation into several pollution sites near his home in southwestern Alberta.

I asked Andy recently whether he could see much cause for hope now as the 21st century begins. He stared off into space for a few moments before answering. "I think we're over the hump. I think we raised enough hell that they're going to be awful careful about what they'll try and pull off. I mean, some of the stuff government and the oil companies pulled off back in the late '50s and '60s and '70s was totally against the law. But now they're getting so they're having to kind of think about breaking the law. They didn't pay any attention to their own laws at all in the old days."

Almost a century ago some of Bert Riggall's regular clients built a rustic lodge on one of the highest points on his ranch, a place he called Hawk's Nest Butte after a pair of red-tailed hawks who nested regularly near its base. At first it served as a summer resort for four Minneapolis families who hired Riggall's outfitting services each summer. Later, it became a summer home for the Russell family.

From the front porch of Hawk's Nest, the view is staggering. Away south stands Chief Mountain, cliff-walled and aloof, one of the most sacred mountains in Blackfoot culture. A sweep of lesser mountains extends from the Chief in a broad arc west and then north. Beyond their peaks is the promise of remote, wilder country: the upper Castle drainage, the vast Flathead Valley and, farther north, the upper Oldman. Below, a mosaic of aspen and fescue grassland sprawls peacefully down Cottonwood Creek, past century-old ranches, to the boundary of Waterton Lakes National Park.

This is all grizzly country, and it's all Andy Russell country. The fact that grizzlies still survive here after having been extirpated from so much of their North American range, and the persistence here of so much wild habitat after a century of pell-mell habitat destruction, both stand as tribute to the unending energy, remarkable storytelling and determined activism of one of North America's most famous conservationists.

Andy Russell no longer stands quite as erect as he once did, and his jet-black hair has gone silver. His face remains craggy, but softened with age. His eyes still spark with humour when he holds court for the most recent visitors to Hawk's Nest. In the golden light of another spring evening, as the people gathered on the old wooden porch watch the last streak of golden sunlight fade from the ranchlands spread below, the old man for the mountains leans forward to catch what someone says.

He chuckles and shakes his head. "That reminds me of the time when old Frenchy Rivière was trapping beavers up on the Drywood," he begins, watching faces turn to him, expectant and eager. He leans back and gazes out into the far places of his memory, and chuckles again. Time for another story. Conservation, as always, will follow.

Truly Good People

 loyd Lohr is a quiet man with a deep, abiding love of nature. A farmer who lives near Stettler, now retired, he carefully husbanded his family farm for almost half a century before handing over the reins to the next generation. His grandfather's homestead, now grown in with aspens and wildflowers, is still visible in a half section of wooded land the Lohrs have never cleared or broken. Lloyd watches birds there in summer, and allows a few hunters at a time to pursue whitetails through the quiet woodland each fall.

Like many other farmers, Lloyd safeguards a pocket of habitat that would yield far more income if developed. He does it because he loves wildlife and identifies his own well-being with the health of a landscape of which luck and good planning have made him steward. He puts up bluebird and duck boxes each year and volunteers with local and provincial natural history groups like the Federation of Alberta Naturalists.

Francis and Bonnie Gardner ranch a few hundred kilometres south of Lloyd, near the headwaters of Willow Creek. Francis calls their ranch a "working wilderness." His cattle share the windy foothills ridges with bands of elk and mule deer, grizzly bears and, in recent years, wolves. Although the family has lost cattle to wolves more than once, he bears them no malice. When he has problems, he calls in the Alberta Fish and Wildlife Service to dispose of the offenders. When he has no problems, which is most of the time, he takes pride in the fact that, under his family's stewardship, their ranch remains so wild and healthy that even wolves and grizzly bears can survive there. Not too many miles away a neighbour takes this kind of thinking a step further by even refusing hunters permission to shoot wolves, coyotes or other predators.

The Gardners have won awards for their caring and progressive attitudes toward land health. Farther south, at the head of Todd Creek, Hilton and Alta Pharis have gotten their share of recognition, too. Looking at the gradual degradation their cattle had wrought on the willows and other riparian vegetation along upper Todd Creek, the Pharis' embarked several years ago on a determined mission to restore the health of the stream so that, as Hilton says, "...we could leave things a little better than they were when we got them."

Behind the fences that now guard the most sensitive parts of their stream corridor, sedges and reedgrass grow thick and lush in the gaps among the flourishing willow stands. Cutthroat trout numbers have rebounded and the valley looks vigorous, green and well-loved. Caring shows.

Harvey Locke and Wendy Francis don't own land that they can care for in the way that the Lohrs, Gardners and Pharis' do. Nonetheless, their labour of love shows on Alberta's landscape too. Harvey was born in Lake Louise in Banff National Park. He grew up with a deep personal attachment to the mountain paradise. As years passed, however, he saw the small mountain town of Banff give itself over to uncontrolled commercial activity. Dismayed, he watched as Parks Canada seemed to make no serious effort to slow down the cancerous growth of ski hills and resorts. He determined to do whatever he could to protect Canada's first national park from greed and bungling. Wendy, his wife and a fellow lawyer, was no less committed to saving parks. She resigned from her law firm to become the conservation director of a local chapter of the Canadian Parks and Wilderness Society.

In 1995 Canada's Minister of Canadian Heritage released a new park management plan for Banff that was, to a large extent, the result of Harvey's and Wendy's work. Thanks to their sacrifice of countless volunteer hours, donated dollars and deferred holidays, Banff's frenzied conversion into a scenic shopping mall has been brought to a near halt. Parks Canada is slowly putting the badly impaired Bow River valley in the heart of the park back together by pulling out unnecessary facilities and restoring damaged habitats and movement corridors.

Elliot Fox is a native of Kainaiwa, the Blood Tribe. After he graduated from Lethbridge Community College he began talking to other tribal members about environmental problems and restoration opportunities on the Blood Reserve—Canada's largest. Building on the cultural

value his people have traditionally attached to the earth and its creatures, he and other concerned members of the tribe established an environmental organization to clean up landfills, promote better waste management and fight weed infestations. He developed a resource management plan for the tribe's timber berth to protect its wilderness qualities
and vulnerable wildlife species, while allocating a controlled amount of
timber for cutting. His efforts helped restore a vitally important bull
trout spawning run and have put the Blood Tribe into the front line of
First Nations environmental protection.

Jan Edmonds is a biologist who lives in Edson. She has spent more
than a decade working with government, conservation groups, logging
companies and others to try and ensure the future of west-central Alberta's beleaguered woodland caribou herds. In spite of setbacks—like the
government's allocation of virtually all the region's caribou habitat to
large pulp companies and the failure of Alberta's Special Places program
to deliver anything more than postage-stamp sized pockets of partly
protected habitat—Jan has persevered tirelessly. Eternally positive, she
continues to work every imaginable angle to buy time and habitat for the
old-growth-dependent, and too-easily-poached grey ghosts of the
northern forest.

Lorne Fitch, a fisheries biologist in Alberta Environment's Lethbridge office, has spent more than two decades working to protect biological diversity in the most heavily modified part of the province-the
prairie south. With Barry Adams, another dedicated civil servant from
Alberta Public Lands, Lorne developed the Alberta Riparian Conservation Program, or "Cows and Fish" as it has come to be known. Working
with other conservationists like the Alberta Cattle Commission's Keith
Everts and Chris Mills, and Trout Unlimited's Gary Szabo, as well as a
growing number of ranchers and farmers, Lorne and Barry have revital-
ized countless kilometres of southern Alberta creek bottoms simply by
rearranging the way cows use their watersheds.

From the Alberta Wilderness Association's Dianne Pachal and Cliff
Wallis, the Alberta Fish and Game Association's Darryl Smith and Andy
Boyd, to tireless activist Martha Kostuch, the late conservationist-histo-

rian Grant MacEwan and backyard nature expert Myrna Pearman, Alberta is full of people whose love of land and wildlife burns intensely, fuelling conservation action from Rainbow Lake to Onefour. Hunters donate a few weekends to plant shrubs and trees along irrigation canals. Housewives volunteer to stuff envelopes for wilderness advocacy groups. Scout and 4-H groups do litter blitzes. Farmers leave hayfield corners uncut. None expect praise—they just want to keep things good, or make them better. Love motivates them, not greed, self-interest or political ambition.

These are truly good people. In their devotion to nurturing and restoring the ecological diversity that is Alberta, they demonstrate that the 20th century produced more than environmental harm. It also bred a new kind of Albertan: people who choose to cherish and defend their home, rather than exploiting it like strangers. These are our neighbours and friends, and they are among this province's most valuable natural resources. Their quiet dedication enriches us all.

God bless them, every one.

Home Range

Becoming Native

I was attending a conference in Waterton Lakes National Park the day the lake came in the door. Surrounded with flip charts and projection screens, hypnotized by the drone of speaker after speaker, nobody was really conscious of how heavily the rain was falling outside. By mid-afternoon, 23 centimetres had fallen and Waterton Lake began to sneak under the doors of the meeting room, long puddles snaking under chairs and into shoes.

The rising water had already become so deep that, as we evacuated the conference participants across the causeway at the head of Emerald Bay late that afternoon, waves washed over the hoods of pickup trucks. When the conference reconvened in Lethbridge later that day, the flood crest was at Lethbridge and there was some concern that the highway bridge could wash out. The whole valley was wall-to-wall water, with only the tops of the cottonwoods sticking out.

That flood of 1995 rearranged a lot of southern Alberta's landscape, as floods have always done from time to time. Among the many changes the churning brown waters wrought was to wash out the bottom ends of several alluvial fans along Blakiston Creek valley. Near Crandell Lake Campground, the new flood scars exposed old bones from long-dead bison.

Scientists trying to assemble an ecological history of the foothills have debated for many years about the bison that used to winter along the foot of the Rockies. Some of the written accounts left by early European explorers described two kinds of bison: the plains bison and the mountain bison. Mountain bison were supposed to be taller, wider-horned animals that summered up around timberline and in the high valleys, then wintered down in the grassy foothills where they mingled with much larger numbers of bison from out on the prairies. Some ecological historians scoff at the idea of the mountain bison ever existing, but others swear it's true and they have the remains to prove it.

Old bones washed out halfway between the foothills and the head-waters would likely be mountain bison, so an analysis of those bones might help settle the question. The chemical content of those bones is bound to reflect the chemical contents of bison foods, after all, and mountain bison would have had different diets than those that lived on the plains.

Most plants turn carbon from carbon dioxide into organic carbon by one of two different metabolic pathways. C4 plants are extremely efficient, but to process carbon they need long, hot growing seasons; the C4 pathway demands a lot of heat energy. C3 plants are less efficient, but they can grow in cooler conditions. The carbon isotopes produced by each pathway are different, so by analysing carbon in the bones of plant-eating animals scientists can find out if they ate mostly C4 plants or C3.

Canada, being a relatively cool place, has few C4 plants. Fortuitously, however, one of the most common C4 plants is blue grama, a low-growing curly grass that happens to be a favourite food of plains bison. Only C3 plants live in the Rockies.

If those bones in Blakiston Creek had only C3 carbon isotopes, that would be compelling proof that they came from mountain bison that never got out onto the plains. On the other hand, if there were C4 carbon isotopes, then these must have been plains bison at some point. That, in fact, is what the researchers who looked at Blakiston Creek bison bones found. Although they didn't prove beyond a doubt that no mountain bison ranged the prehistoric Rockies, they did prove that plains bison once ranged that far upvalley.

Other researchers have looked at other chemicals in body tissues. Their studies show that the same principle applies elsewhere. An animal's body has the same chemical isotopes as the plants that grow in its home habitat, and as other animals that live in the same place. All are processing the same local materials through interconnected food chains, after all. God made Adam, Genesis tells us, from a pinch of dust. Adam was made of the very stuff of the place he lived. It makes sense. So are other local creatures rooted in and derived from the places of their lives.

What, then, might scientists find if they were to try to figure out where we lived by analysing our body tissues? The chemicals in our bodies come from Brazilian coffee, California vegetables, Manitoba wheat, Atlantic cod, anywhere beef—ultimately, we cannot be chemically traced to any home landscape. Our bones contain chemical graffiti, not the signature of a place where we can say we belong. They betray our rootlessness, our lack of belonging—our ecological promiscuity.

I suspect that this placelessness and unrootedness that have come to characterize North American culture are the bottom line, in many ways, of the modern environmental crisis. And if that is so, then the need for roots and belonging should be the point of aim for anyone engaged in environmental education. Too often, educators build curricula and technique on the same flawed underpinnings as the problems they are designed to address. We need to dig deeper if environmental education is to be effective at addressing the root causes of our cultural dysfunction.

Wallace Stegner was writing of the American west, but he might as well have been describing western society in general, when he said:

> Our migratoriness has hindered us from becoming a people of communities and traditions, especially in the West. It has robbed us of the gods who make places holy. It has cut off individuals and families and communities from memory and the continuum of time. It has left at least some of us with a kind of spiritual pellagra, a deficiency disease, a hungering for the ties of a rich and stable social order. Not only is the American home a launching pad, as Margaret Mead said; the American community, especially in the West, is an overnight camp. American individualism, much celebrated and cherished, has developed without its essential corrective, which is belonging. Freedom, when found, can turn out to be airless and unsustaining. Especially in the West, what we have instead of place is space. Place is more than half memory, shared memory. Rarely do Westerners stay long enough at one stop to share much of anything.

How many of us live today in the town in which we were born? How many of us turn regularly to our community elders for counsel? How many of us know the stories of our present landscapes: the secret places, who planted the old windbreak just there, or why the hillside slumped, and when?

Like the bison in Blakiston Valley, there used to be people who lived here and were defined by this place. They had no choice; they lacked the kinds of transportation technology and fossil fuels that enable us today to walk away from bad decisions. If one were to examine the bones of a Piikanii or K'tunaxa person from a couple centuries ago, one would find the same chemical isotopes, in the same proportions, as in those bison bones, or in the landscape itself. All were of this place; all, ultimately, were the same thing.

Those people must have known this place intimately; all its stories and much of its history. They went often and always to their elders for counsel and advice, because those elders represented decades of successful survival in the same world in which younger generations must grow up. These were people who coexisted with dangerous predators like grizzly bears and cougars. They hunted large, powerful and migratory prey. They used fire—a terrifying force. They had no alternative but to live with the consequences of their choices, so the traditional knowledge of their elders was vitally important to them.

Our elders, on the other hand, generally end up marginalized and irrelevant. We put them in homes. We think of ourselves as having to provide for them; we don't see them providing essential knowledge and wisdom to us. Why? Because the world they learned their life skills in has passed; they and we changed it. We don't live at home now anyway. The past means little to us compared with the future: we embrace change and movement as not only normal but essential. We are forever leaving home and cutting ties, in our quests for future success.

When place-based people—like the aboriginal people who lived here before smallpox, guns and lawyers—change the landscape, they must live with those changes. So they make changes they can live with. If they fail, they suffer. If they ruin some resource, they die. This kind of dependence focuses the mind. In fact, there were probably far fewer waking moments in the life of a pre-contact aboriginal when he or she wasn't thinking about the nature of their home place than there is in ours. We've got other stuff to think about: interest rates, the latest conflict in the Middle East, computer upgrades, next week's to-do list, whatever. Little of it is place-based.

If we make a mess of the place where we live, we can just move on. The town gets too crowded or the landscape too full of acreages—just sell and find a place less crowded. Exhaust the soil—import some fertilizer. Run out of cod—switch to haddock. Overhunt the bears—plan your next hunt for northern B.C. Pollute the water supply—build a pipeline farther upstream.

And so we have become lost in a world we have ceased to know. We are orphaned; we continually orphan ourselves, by choice, from nature. We live as perpetual outsiders who view the world far more often as an objective, external reality—hence the term "environment," that which surrounds—than as a subjective thing that defines us and gives us meaning as human beings.

The social mission of environmental education, then, must be to take a society of promiscuous outsiders and build it into a culture of native people—to marry us to our homes. I call it a social mission deliberately, because I believe that environmental education, at its best, can speak to a deep, fundamental need for belonging in all of us. We don't like being rootless. We don't want to be adrift. We want to know who we are; who we really are. But we only vaguely, and rarely, contemplate or understand what keeps us so disconnected.

Being native, in my view, is to identify oneself with one's place. Once you see bunchgrass slopes, windy pine ridges, coyotes, curlews and clear-bottomed creeks as part of who you are as a person, you can no longer respond with objective coldness to things that might harm those. Why are environmentalists so often accused of being emotional by the placeless, objective entities that seek to change and degrade landscapes we love? Because we *are* emotional, in a deeply fundamental way: we see ourselves in the things they threaten.

That's how it should be. Psychologists have a name for people who succeed in being coldly objective and free of emotional engagement: they call them psychopaths. Psychopaths consider abusive cruelty to be rational so long as it meets their personal needs—a point worth pondering when looking at the signs of abuse that scar our western landscapes. Only those who choose to remain outsiders can isolate themselves emotionally from the fate of the land and its wildlife; those who choose to belong, cannot.

Being native is adapting self to place, rather than place to self. In a cold country, it might mean learning to like turnips and cabbage rather than trying to grow tomatoes and corn. In a dry land, it might mean choosing to conserve water, rather than choking rivers with dams to create the illusion of abundance. In any land, it must mean pondering long, even agonizing, over anything that might change the nature of that place and in so doing change our own meanings as people.

Being native means owning the history of our home places, anchoring ourselves in tradition, and valuing the wisdom and experience of those whose relationships with our home places reach back farther than ours. It means rediscovering the meaning of elders. It means building conservation through community, not in spite of it.

Being native, in short, means choosing to live as if we intend to stay—because we do intend to stay. Because moving on would be an admission of failure, and an abandonment of self.

It is not easy, however, to become native in a world of bluegrass lawns, vinyl siding, 7-Elevens, Microsoft and consumer culture. Yet we call ourselves western, we say we are Albertans; we name ourselves after these places. Why is that? And what are these places, then? It may not be easy to become native, but most of us feel a deep-rooted need to do so. And if there is any hope for us and the places where we live, then we need to acquire nativeness somehow.

This suggests to me that environmental education should not be about "green living": generic, placeless ways of reducing one's impact by recycling, vermiposting or whatever. It should certainly not be built around corporation-funded materials that deal with broad themes like water management or forestry instead of specific places, and that promote, however subtly, a vested interest in exploitation. Nor should it focus on environmental issues: educating youth about global climate change and ozone thinning and persistent contaminants in the environment. These are placeless approaches that speak to students out of the same objective, technology-will-save-us-tomorrow, "the environment is out there" perspective that generates so much ecological dysfunction in the first place. These approaches may have secondary value but, like framing, dry-walling and finishing, the first priority must be to build a strong foundation of belonging.

How might those of us who educate children about their environment build the foundations of nativeness? We can do it only by creating opportunities for children to bond to their home places. Perhaps no less important, we need to devise ways of linking them to local elders who know the stories of those places. Nativeness is about place-bonding and self-identity: the most meaningful achievements of a well-lived childhood. The 21st century will build a sustaining, native culture not by putting great resources on the Internet or bringing wonderful environmental curriculum materials into the classroom, but by putting children out into the real living world long enough, and often enough, that they begin to see their own identities reflecting back from their surroundings.

Local elders include aboriginal elders, retired farmers and ranchers, retirement home residents. Communities used to provide many ways by which elders and children could interact; we need to devise new ways to replace what we lost in the chaos of the 20th century. Family history projects trace genealogies back to other places by connecting children to their family elders. Perhaps now we could encourage schoolchildren to do "place history" projects by consulting with community elders who know the histories of buildings, fields, rivers or local landscapes. At its best, environmental education could help recreate the role of the community elder in passing on knowledge of home and of local life-ways to younger generations.

The most powerful place-bonding experiences in my own life came from wandering the landscape alone or with a respected elder like my father. Birdwatching trips with the Calgary Bird Club played an important role because of generous men and women who were willing to put up with the enthusiasm of kids they weren't related to. So did hunting and fishing, because they immersed me in landscape and engaged my imagination and intelligence in trying to figure it out and relate to it. Environmental educators, whether in homes, schools or the community, need to find ways to take or send children into the wild where they can fill themselves with the kinds of sensations, insights and feelings that come only from personal exploration and discovery. Children can't be expected to take personal responsibility for the well-being of the living world, until they can find their identities not through their clothing styles, possessions, sports teams or the Internet, but through the real living world of nature and community.

Field trip money, however, is scarce in modern school budgets. Group experience of nature is generally a poor substitute for personal discovery, however, so this is not necessarily bad news. Creative teachers already get around the lack of field trip time by assigning tasks and explorations for students to undertake on their own time. Find 10 kinds of bird and describe in words or pictures their flight or gait, or how they behave near people. Select five individual plants and keep a journal on when their buds swell, leaves burst or flowers appear. Homework need not be inside a house: where is "home," anyway?

Whatever the case, the best environmental education will always be built on local, place-specific information rather than packaged, generic materials. It accomplishes little to teach children about agriculture in general. What they most need to know is what crops grow in their home place and how their home community has interacted with local fields and farmlands over the years. Meaningful consideration of agriculture as part of their local culture might lead to consideration of which elements of their home farmscapes they might most want to sustain so that they can continue to feel at home there.

The most powerful force for sustainability and a healthy environment has always been passionately engaged individuals and communities. Recent history has shown that those who most advance the causes of wilderness protection, ecological restoration, sustainable agriculture, healthy communities and environmental protection are people who care passionately and personally about their home places. These are people whose lives have been formed within nature and landscape, who could no sooner give up on the well-being of their home places than they could allow others to hurt their children or disfigure themselves. These are people who cannot distinguish between self and environment. These, fundamentally, are native people. The land lives inside their very bones, as it did inside the bones of those bison; as it does inside the bones of all native creatures.

The Home Stream

It took half a lifetime of fishing to teach me one very simple piece of angling wisdom: don't chase good fishing. I would have learned it earlier, but frontier fishing dulled my brain.

I came to fishing in the early 1960s, a time when oil companies were cutting seismic lines and new roads into every lonely trout stream in western Alberta. It was an extravagant and wasteful era, and wild Alberta is poorer today because of it, but it certainly made for rich explorations.

Each year my older brother Gordon and I would help Dad pore over his dogeared maps and find unfamiliar streams we could explore by following new seismic lines. Sometimes the fishing was great. Other times it wasn't. If it wasn't, we went looking for another stream.

Even then, I now realize with the clarity of hindsight, the beginnings of wisdom were there. Certain streams—Elk Creek, the upper Elbow River, Threepoint Creek—drew us faithfully back every second year when they opened for fishing. These were the places whose names eventually became woven into family legend. It was like coming home to break out of the pines into the little valley of Barbershop Creek and see it winking at us like an old friend as it meandered through its long meadow of bunchgrass, shooting stars and dwarf birch. Along those streams we could say things like, "Meet me for lunch at the pool where Gordon fell in that time," or "I caught two in the big bull trout hole."

But Gordon and I, more than my Dad, remained convinced that we were sure to find even better fishing if we just pushed the family station wagon a little harder and hiked a little farther to another of the mysterious little wiggles on Dad's old maps. We left the familiar streams behind after one or two visits, and ventured on in search of the holy angling grail.

It was a promiscuous kind of fishing, the kind that comes naturally in a frontier civilization where it seems like everyone takes chances, explores the unknown and hopes for a big find.

It didn't help any when I found my first copy of the Alberta Fishing Guide sitting on the counter in Webber's Hardware one spring when I went there to stock up on salmon eggs and snelled flies.

"Dad, listen," I'd say to my harried father as we bounced and jolted up the Forestry Trunk Road, breathing shallowly so as not to choke on the road dust that poured into the car, "'Tay River, bull trout to 10 pounds, brown trout to four.' Please, Dad, we've got to try the Tay River!"

So we'd try the Tay River, and catch bull trout to 10 inches, brown trout to zero. And no sooner would we get back to the car than I'd be flipping pages again. Dad would try and stash the fishing guide out of sight and entice us off to some stream we already knew—but we wanted to catch big ones in exotic places. Today I still have to fight that impulse to look for strange creek names and seductive promises when I open each year's new edition.

Compounding the temptation are the "Where to Go" columns that now grace end-of-week editions of Alberta's daily newspapers. Saturday morning, dozens of anglers hit the pavement following the promise of hot fishing on the Crowsnest River, Elbow Lake, the lower Bow or the Fallen Timber—wherever it is that this week's column promises clearing water, good hatches and excellent action on San Juan worms or some other favoured lure.

For many years Bruce Masterman wrote a weekly column for an Alberta daily newspaper in which he advised readers where to find good fishing. But as the next generation of aspiring young anglers nagged their parents to take them out to the week's hot spot, few realized that Bruce was likely taking his own offspring out to one of only a small number of favourite fishing streams. The little mountain meadow stream where native cutthroats rise eagerly each summer afternoon; a back channel of the Highwood River where little brookies haunt a series of beaver dams; a brown trout stream so secret that its name never appeared in his column. Wild goose chases don't figure prominently in the personal itinerary of seasoned angling writers like Masterman.

Jim McLennan's classic Blue-Ribbon Bow could not have been written by a man who dropped in casually from time to time between prospecting expeditions to distant streams. Few anglers know as much as McLennan about how to fish the Bow, because few have spent as much time working out its mysteries. By the same token, few care as deeply about its future, because few have formed as deep and lasting a bond to this unique and special place.

There are a whole lot of streams out there and the fishing was always good in some of them last week. Aspiring anglers race off into the sunrise to flirt with a new love for a day or two, before becoming disgruntled and seeking elsewhere for the mother lode. By the end of the summer, they are rarely much further ahead than they were at the beginning, and they remain citizens of no place in particular. Even if they arrived at one or two good spots at the right time, the odds are they aren't the ones who caught all the fish. The good fishing went to anglers who had taken the time to learn how to fish those streams.

There is a cure for this madness. It comes to some of us with age, as knees and energy levels begin to give out. Others come to it earlier, with the result that they enjoy better fishing for more of their lives. It is simply this: pick your home stream, and fish there as often as you can. Fish there when the fishing is bad. Fish there when the fishing is good. Don't stop, don't wander and, in time, the fishing will become better. And so will you.

I'm a slow learner. I never woke up to this simple truth until a few years ago, when Gail and I mortgaged our future to buy some land near a small river in southern Alberta. I had fished it three times before, between trips to virtually everywhere. It was great one time and forgettable the other two. But once we got into the serious business of building a cabin, tending a garden, and making time for our kids in their own new place, I found that I didn't have a lot of spare time left for exploring all the many other creeks, rivers and lakes in the surrounding country. I live only 40 minutes from the famed Crowsnest River, and haven't fished it for five years. Police Outpost and Beauvais Lakes are close by, as are the tailwaters below the Oldman River Dam. I ignore them all. It might be years before I get around to them, because the more time I spend on the home river, the more I realize I have left to figure out.

It took two seasons to find the runs where giant, weighted stonefly nymphs were almost certain to yield large rainbows early in the spring. Still unsolved is the mystery of the pods of trout that feed all through the sultry low-water days of July and August in the long run upstream from the cabin. One afternoon I watched from a clifftop with binoculars as they cruised lazily about, rising and sipping, turning, rising and sipping. There was no point in casting to them; they'd ignored all my flies already. I suspect that they were eating tiny *Trichorythodes* mayflies; I will have to find the coordination and patience to tie Number 22 flies some day. Then I'll have to figure out how to fish them, which will almost certainly take many weeks and many tippets. No problem; I have the time.

Fishing that same stretch of river has forced me to solve problems through perseverance, not by walking away from them. One right-angle bend in the river is a miserable chaos of cross-currents, upwellings and boulders. Brian, at nine years old, was a hardware fisherman by necessity; this pool is now known among the family as "The pool where Brian caught the big bull trout" —his second fish ever—but it stymied me until last spring. The deep water on the inside of the bend tantalized me for months, but I couldn't drift a fly into it without crosscurrents wrenching it out of position.

After much frustration, I discovered that by inching out at the edge of the tail I could follow a gravel bar into the foam and get into a position from which it was possible to lob a weighted stonefly nymph into the head of the run. From there, I could follow its float down into the eddy without having a powerful boil lift my line and fly to the surface. Brian's pool, it turns out, holds big rainbows as well as big bull trout. And I was pretty pleased with myself that it took only three years to figure out how to catch them.

Barry Mitchell, publisher of the Alberta Fishing Guide, finds himself, from time to time, sharing a riverbank with an inexperienced angler who hopes to learn more. "Without exception," says Barry, "I tell them that the number one thing is not to skip all over the country in search of trout, but to pick out one or two streams and spend the next couple years fishing there and nowhere else."

Mitchell admits that a lot of people look askance, and too few follow his advice. But, he insists, "The hardest thing about learning how to catch fish is learning how to read water. Each stream is different, so if you keep moving around you're never going to learn properly."

Mitchell's insight dates back to 1975 when, after working in B.C. for a number of years, he moved back to Alberta and settled in Red Deer. He knew of Stauffer Creek's reputation for abundant, large brown trout, and began fishing it regularly that year. He had little luck; most of his fly-fishing experience was on B.C. lakes and he had never fished running water for browns before.

"It wasn't until the middle of August a year later that I finally caught my first trout out of Stauffer Creek," he says. "And the only reason I caught it was that I'd become virtually obsessed. If I'd acted like everyone else I would have given up long ago and headed over the hill to the next creek.

"I didn't realize what I had done until the early 1980s. I would take other guys out there and of course I'd catch trout and they wouldn't. I'd never see those guys on Stauffer Creek again even though the fishing was better than ever. That was when I realized how important it is to spend a lot of time getting to know one stream and work out the problems of how to fish it."

Slowly, I've been getting to know our family's home stream. I'm still a long way from working out all the problems of how to fish it. But as I wade its riffles or pick my way along its gravel bars, studying on these problems, it becomes increasingly clear that there are more benefits to concentrating on a favourite stream than simply becoming a better angler. Gail and I need only listen to the chatter of our children each evening to realize that.

The kids know our home river better than I ever got to know the streams of my youth. They know the place where the mink often hunt early in the morning. They know the deer crossings, the good hiding places for spying on passing anglers and the places where the most baby poplars sprouted after the big flood of 1995. They remember how the whitefish pool looked before the flood, after which it became Katie's beach. When we stop to look at the old beaver stumps, they reminisce how there was a deep channel there before the big flood built a new gravel bar and pushed the river channel over 100 metres to where the goose family spent the spring.

We had just begun to feel we knew our home river when the big flood came down in 1995. Now we have new pools, new boulder runs and new mysteries. The fox den is buried under a foot of new sand, but we remember it. Gail and I know the weed patches, and our backs remember well the hours spent pulling them while the kids fished nearby. We know the bank where the sand lilies surprised us with their waxy blossoms and tropical scent one summer evening when nighthawks boomed overhead and rainbows rose feverishly all along the edge of the cliff pool.

Getting to know a home stream intimately takes time and commitment, just like any other worthwhile relationship. But it pays off not only in better fishing, but greater depth of experience. We're a mobile society; by the time we are grown few of us live in the same community where we were born. Our lives aren't tied to place the way those of earlier generations were. A friend once told me that most people are orphaned from nature.

My children aren't. They have a home stream. I think that's going to serve them better, in the years to come, than the frenzied explorations of my childhood. I know for sure that they are far better anglers than I was at their ages.

I suspect that choosing a favourite stream or reach of river, and returning to it season after season and year after year offers an antidote to the rootlessness of the late 20th century. The familiar lap of a familiar stream on well-known cobbles, the flash of a nymphing trout where you caught the half-metre-long rainbow last year during a hatch of caddisflies, the remains of last-year's robin nest in the leaning alder: each visit builds on the last and ties you more intimately to the place, and the stream and the fish who dwell there.

One does not simply go fishing on such a river; one comes home.

The Once and Future Wild

The 20th century seemed to recede behind us as the current bore us steadily down into the wild Milk River canyon. Plains cottonwoods-ragged trees with massive trunks-blushed green along the river banks. Swallows skimmed between the boats. The air smelled of brown river water, sage and balsam. The canyon walls, soft curves and bleached lines, receded up toward the sky across broad sagebrush flats.

Gail dipped her paddle lazily into the gentle current. Brian, our two year old, slept on her lap. Katie, bright-eyed with interest, gripped the gunwales and peered back upriver.

I glanced back too. I could see Corey, our oldest boy, perched in the bow of Ian Jack's big rowboat. Closer by, Mike McIvor, bushy-bearded and craggy-faced, pointed out a kingfisher to his wife Diane. Ahead, two more canoes were just disappearing around a bend.

As I turned back and straightened out the canoe, an immense slab of riverbank, easily seven metres high, calved off and crashed into the river only a few metres ahead of us. The pool erupted in a great foam of brown water that set our canoe rocking. We floated over the place where the bank had disappeared, but there was no sign that anything had happened. The river had eaten several cubic metres of silt and not even burped.

Gail said, "That could have hit us!"

I nodded, shocked by the suddenness with which the bank had collapsed, and the eerie finality with which the river had swallowed up all traces of the cave-in. It was a reminder that this place was as close to wilderness as anywhere in Canada's prairie landscape.

The Milk River Canyon is in extreme southeastern Alberta-closer to Regina than to Calgary. The river's tortuous meanders trace green scrollwork along the bottom of one of the deepest and broadest canyons in prairie Canada. Looming like mirages, the towering cones of Montana's Sweetgrass Hills rise above the canyon's southern rim. To the north, if one is willing to spend an hour or two hiking up eroded slopes-dodging clumps of prickly pear cactus and keeping a sharp eye out for rattlesnakes—a gently undulating expanse of mixed grassland sweeps away to the flanks of the Cypress Hills: some of the finest surviving native prairie in Canada.

Canada's prairies have lost 90 percent of their native vegetation and contain half the country's endangered species. Even the Milk River canyon's vast expanse of prairie, badlands and river bottom is a pale shadow of what it used to be. Bison no longer drown by the hundreds each spring when crossing the swollen river. No grizzly bears scavenge on bison carcasses in spring, or fatten on chokecherries and saskatoon berries each fall in the shrubby coulees that drain down to the Milk. As shadows spill purple across the sagebrush flats and nighthawks begin to call above the cottonwoods, the scalp-tightening howl of lobo wolves no longer shocks the evening into listening stillness.

The occasional distant rumble does not herald the approach of tens of thousands of bison but merely the passage, high overhead, of another passenger jet. The scenery is spectacular, but strangely empty. Like other places modern Canadians perceive as wilderness, the Milk River canyon retains its scenic beauty but has lost much of its ecological wealth.

Canada has little of its original wilderness left. The 20th century was too brash; we were all in too much of a hurry. Even the great barren lands of the Inuit and other northern peoples are marked by abandoned camps and new diamond mines; the very permafrost is melting as the global climate warms. Other regions retain little at all of the wild-southern Ontario's Carolinian forests survive only as tiny tatters, for example. In most of Canada the wild is wounded and under threat.

With the exception of the children, all the people floating down the Milk River that June day in 1991 were experienced in the art of making do with wounded wilderness. The McIvors had spent two decades fighting to save Banff National Park's shrinking wilds from encroaching commercialism. Ian Jack had campaigned almost as long to keep BC Hydro from destroying the last undammed stretch of the Columbia River. Rob and Corlane Gardner, from Medicine Hat, Alberta, worked daily to save prairie Canada's last remnants from a host of assaults. All were familiar with the taste of defeat.

Today, we floated through a wilderness of ghosts, concentrating on that which still survived rather than letting our minds linger on what might have been. The Milk River canyon was the kind of setting that made it almost possible to forget what we all knew: that Canada's future nature would never be as wild or complete as its past.

And then we saw the elk.

It was late afternoon when the first boat swung past a logjam and slipped around a bend, dipping into a sudden riffle. Someone pointed. Paddles stilled. Everyone watched, as we floated quietly down the length of a long pool toward four elk who stood hock deep in the tail of the pool.

They were sleek and dark in their new summer coats. They looked strangely huge. Eight ears were cocked toward the approaching boats, eyes wide, nostrils flaring. Then the nearest cow barked and wheeled, and all four thundered up out of the river in a spray of foam. Noses held high in characteristic elk fashion, they vanished into the cottonwood forest.

We floated in close to shore. I could see water seeping into their tracks—elk tracks, beside the Milk River. Nobody spoke. None of us had imagined that elk might find their way back into this relict prairie wilderness after having been eradicated more than half a century earlier. It was a profound epiphany; all sense of loss and reluctant compromise spontaneously erased. That evening I found myself glassing the cottonwood flats and canyon slopes, half-believing I might see a grizzly digging roots.

Lately, I hear that over 200 elk now range through the Milk River canyon. Two years ago, only a few kilometres away, a pair of wolves appeared out of nowhere, denned and raised a litter of pups.

Prevailing wisdom about Canada's diminishing wilds says that elk and wolves are gone from the prairies forever, but that prevailing wisdom is proving wrong. In the same way, against all hope, trumpeter swans, sandhill cranes and otters have found their way back into the windy aspen parkland of southwestern Alberta where I lived for many years, and the once endangered bald eagle and peregrine falcon again trace graceful lines across southern Ontario skies. The wild, against all logic, has begun to return.

The baby boom generation, my generation, grew up trying to suppress our belief that the wilderness that in so many ways defines Canada was doomed ultimately to vanish. When Kurt Vonnegut wrote, "Things are going to keep on getting worse and worse and never get better again," we knew he was right. We knew that pulp companies, big oil, agro-industry and urbanization would win in the long run, and that wilderness, like clean air, was something we must resign ourselves to leaving behind. We thought we would have to be content with the leavings—the little bits we could wrestle out of industry's grasp and horde for future generations of Canadians.

Now, at the dawn of a new millennium, I think we were wrong. I think Canadians have already begun to bring back the wild. Wilderness is not just part of our past; it will be an important part of our future. We have not surrendered hope; we are reinventing it.

That magical encounter with an animal once eradicated from Canada's prairies had a hidden significance that eluded me until much later. It wasn't until the fall of 1997, when I returned to sit on the edge of the Milk River canyon and look down at its scrolling patterns of cottonwoods, thorny buffaloberry and needlegrass meadows, that I began to see the profound significance of that brief encounter.

It was October. The cottonwoods were golden. Wind hissed and whispered in the grass around me as I sat on the edge of a sandstone cliff and watched my children explore the tangled shrubbery below. The far river was shrunken and pale, winking in and out of sight amid the trees. An eagle looped slowly across the sky.

Contemplating the times I'd been here before, I realized that my life had spanned most of the last half of the 20th century. The children whose happy voices lifted every so often on the wind would live most of their lives in the next. And I realized, suddenly, that I no longer felt the same deep foreboding about their future that had haunted me when we embarked on that float trip seven years earlier. During the last years of the 20th century unimagined possibilities, once rare as prairie elk, began to emerge out of the gloom, offering growing hope that we can yet restore much of the wildness that Canada has lost.

Mike and Diane McIvor's tireless efforts on behalf of Canada's first national park finally bore fruit in 1995 when Canada's Minister of Environment released the report of a scientific panel that had conducted an independent review of how Parks Canada was managing the Banff Bow Valley. The Banff Bow Valley study proved beyond any remaining doubt that the McIvors had been right all along. The following year, Parks Canada announced a new management plan for Banff National Park and began to tear down tourist facilities, restrict travel on some roads and trails, and build bridges and underpasses to help wolves and grizzlies cross the highway.

None of us had even dared believe such a thing was possible, that day in 1991 when we all floated down the Milk River, contemplating the fate of wilderness in the 20th century. Bureaucratic rationalizing and business lobbying had always trumped the efforts of average Canadians who loved the dwindling wild. Nothing hinted that would ever change-but in the last years of the decade it did. The battle for the ecological health of Canada's national parks is far from over, but a new generation of park management plans modelled on Banff's shows that the tide has begun to turn.

In 1995, Rob and Corlane Gardner saw their efforts rewarded too, with the establishment of a new National Wildlife Area along the South Saskatchewan River. Against all established wisdom, Canada's Armed Forces not only supported but actively promoted grassland protection and restoration. Elsewhere in prairie Canada ranchers tired of criticism about the damage their cattle do to riparian areas-the green ribbons of life along streams and rivers-teamed up in the late 1990s with conservation groups and government experts to launch "Cows and Fish," one of the most successful ecosystem restoration programs of the century. All across Rob and Corlane's beloved prairie landscape, new grazing strategies are bringing back willows, clean water and wildlife to once-wounded riparian areas.

Ian Jack, too, after a campaign that lasted almost 30 years, finally secured protection for the last undammed reach of B.C.'s Columbia River: 160 kilometres of cottonwood forest, cattail marsh, oxbow lakes and meandering river stretching from Invermere B.C. north to the sawmill town of Donald. He died shortly after his unimaginable victory, leaving a legacy of hope for future generations out of his own often-hopeless struggles.

All this and more had happened in the few short years since we had come together to enjoy a few days together on one of Canada's last prairie wilderness rivers. There had been no lack of determination among that little group; but there had been a pronounced lack of optimism. We had become conditioned to failure.

Almost from its beginnings Canada's conservation movement was a gloomy one, haunted by the spectres of paradises lost and driven by a kind of crisis mentality. Wilderness protection campaigns were mostly rearguard actions driven by imminent threats: a mine proposal, a tourism development scheme or a new forest allocation. To express optimism or confidence was almost considered a betrayal of values in a movement that drew its desperate energy from an underlying defeatism.

Nonetheless, a people's vision of its future is as subject to reinterpretation as its myths about its past. In Canada, as elsewhere in the world, conservationists increasingly describe the new century in terms of ecosystem restoration and the "re-wilding" of overexploited landscapes. Dialogue about wilderness conservation in the 21st century is no longer dominated by the language of loss, but by the language of healing and recovery.

None speak that language with more quiet passion and commitment than Dave Sheppard.

A gentle, soft-spoken former biology professor, Dave retired from the University of Saskatoon in 1977 and moved to the foothills west of Pincher Creek, Alberta. There he and his wife Jean began to explore the spectacular mountain landscape that lies at the head of the Castle and Carbondale rivers. Originally part of Waterton Lakes National Park, the area contains a host of rare plants, hundreds of elk, deer and bighorn sheep, vitally important habitat for grizzlies and some of the most beautiful streams and mountains in the Canadian Rockies.

As they explored the unexpected paradise that lay just beyond their back door, the Sheppards began to encounter others who shared their growing passion for the place. They also found a growing network of natural gas pipelines, roads and wells. Clearcut logging spread farther into the headwater basins each winter. Noisy dirt bikes and off-road vehicles penetrated everywhere in summer, even onto the summit ridges of some mountains.

Dave Sheppard teamed up in 1990 with others concerned about the thoughtless damage they could see accumulating on the landscape, and formed an advocacy group called the Castle-Crown Wilderness Coalition. Their objective: to persuade the Alberta government to protect the high country as a wilderness park.

But it isn't wilderness, any more than the Milk River canyon is wilderness. Roads penetrate nearly to the head of every valley. Much of the old-growth timber has been clearcut. Gas wells and pumping stations extend up to timberline on some mountains.

Dave Sheppard knows all that but it doesn't deter him. He sees it as wilderness tomorrow, even if it isn't today. He isn't prepared to settle pragmatically for the last few valleys where roads have not yet penetrated; he wants to close roads, reclaim gas well sites, start over again. He believes the land deserves no less. Already the coalition he founded has tasted the first hint of future success; the Alberta government announced in 1997 that it was restricting motor vehicle use on about 80 percent of the roads in what Sheppard and others are already calling the Castle Wilderness again. It's the first sign that the tide of wilderness destruction has begun to ebb.

Dave Sheppard was not among the battle-weary souls who floated the Milk River with my family back in 1991. He was there, however, the next time we all met in one place. It was at the first international conference of the Yellowstone to Yukon conservation initiative, held in the fall of 1997 a couple hundred kilometres west of the Milk River, in Waterton Lakes National Park. Mike and Diane McIvor were among the crowd of more than 400 excited conservationists who gathered to plan the re-wilding of the entire Rocky Mountain chain. So was Rob Gardner. The talk was not about defensive tactics to save the bits that remain; it was about restoring wildness and landscape health to a vast area that suffered too much shortsighted development in the 20th century. There was new energy and new determination on the faces of those people who had met the elk that spring day on the Milk River, and seen their first clue to Canada's wilderness future.

Canada's conservationists are on the offensive at last. While saving what survives of Canada's original wilderness remains important, the emerging ecosystem restoration movement seeks also to restore wildness to places previously written off. Landscapes seemingly lost to development, in this vision, will be the wild green places of tomorrow.

When Shell Canada exhausts the last gas well in Dave Sheppard's much-loved Castle country, the Castle-Crown Wilderness Coalition he helped found will be there to ensure that the company reclaims its well roads. And then a stillness will settle on those valleys. Mystery will seep back out of the woods and shy animals—grizzly bears, elk and wolverine—will venture back into places they have had to avoid for half a century. Those who choose to hike up there will again be able to hear the thin tearing sound that an eagle's wings make when it banks above the whitebark pines and wheels up into the wind. Like the eagle, their eyes, again, will be full of wildness.

By the same token, when Gail's and my children next paddle the Milk River, the elk they see will come as no surprise. In the night they might even hear wolves howl. Perhaps they'll discover fresh grizzly tracks in the river mud. Why not? Why not bison, too? The elk returned. Only lack of imagination and determination stands in the way of rebuilding the living diversity that we once relegated only to our past.

We cannot change our past, but we can choose our future. That future can be better, and wilder, than today. Working together to restore the wild beauty, space, freedom and wildlife that have always shaped our collective dream of Canada, we can heal not just our land but ourselves. Healing, hope, home: in restoring the wild to our native land, we may yet find our way home at last.

The Author

Kevin Van Tighem's roots in Western Canada run deep—his family has lived in this region since 1883. Since he graduated with a Bachelor of Science from the University of Calgary, he has studied wildlife in various western national parks and protected areas. He has written over 200 articles, stories and essays on conservation and wildlife which have won many awards including the Western Magazine Award, the Outdoor Writers of Canada Award and the Journey Award for Fiction. He has served on the executive committee of the Alberta Wilderness Association and the Federation of Alberta Naturalists and has organized two major conferences to promote conservation of rivers and river valleys.

Kevin's other books include *Wild Animals of Western Canada; An Altitude SuperGuide* (1992/1999), *Bears; An Altitude SuperGuide* (1997/1999), *Wild Animals of the Canadian Rockies* (1997), *Coming West; A Natural History of Home* (1997) and *Wild Animals of the American Rockies* (1999).

Kevin is Manager, Ecosystems Secretariat of Jasper National Park. He lives in Jasper with his wife, Gail, and their three children.